W9-BJC-204

ALABAMA

ALABAMA BY ROAD

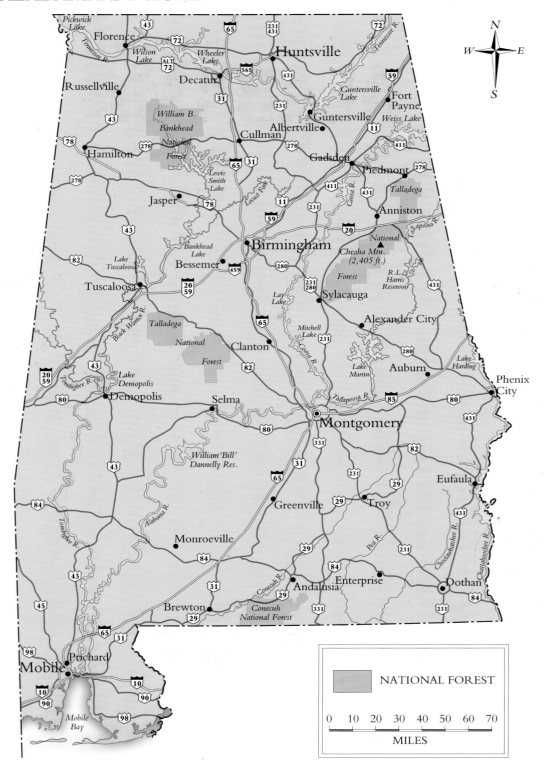

CELEBRATE THE STATES
ALABAMA

David Shirley

BENCHMARK BOOKS

MARSHALL CAVENDISH
NEW YORK

Benchmark Books
Marshall Cavendish Corporation
99 White Plains Road
Tarrytown, New York 10591-9001

Library of Congress Cataloging-in-Publication Data
Shirley, David, date
Alabama / David Shirley.
p.   cm. — (Celebrate the states)
Includes bibiographical references and index.
ISBN 0-7614-0648-4
1. Alabama—Juvenile literature. I. Title. II. Series.
F326.3 .S55   2000   976.1—dc21   99-047250

Maps and graphics supplied by Oxford Cartographers, Oxford, England

Photo Research by Candlepants Incorporated

Cover Photo: Photo Researchers / Jeff Greenberg

The photographs in this book are used by permission and through the courtesy of; *Photo Researchers, Inc.*:
Jeff Lepore, 6-7, back cover; Jeff Greenberg, 10-11, 114-115; Will & Deni McIntyre, 23, 64, 65; M.H. Sharp,
26, 120(bottom); Maslowski, 28; Chromosohm/Joe Sohm, 52-53; Tom Hollyman, 63; Tibor Hirsch, 75;
Will McIntyre, 105; Thomas S. England, 110; Van Bucher, 113; Tom McHugh, 120 (top). *Alabama Bureau of
Tourism & Travel*: Dan Brothers, 13, 19, 135; Karim Shamsi-Basha,74, 76, 82, 98-99, 101, 103, 112, 125.
Corbis: 43, 46; David Muench, 15;Kevin Flemming, 16, 68-69,84-85, 108; Bettmann,41, 48; Bettmann-UPI,
57; Bob Rowan; Progressive Image, 66; Joseph Sohm/ Chromosohm Inc., 71; *William H. Allen Jr.,*: 22, 27
(top), 59, 78, 81, 117, 119, 123. *Animals Animals*: J.H. Robinson, 27(bottom). *Collection of the Birmingham
Museum of Art, Alabama; Gift of Mrs. Elesabeth Ingalls Gillet*: 30-31. *National Museum of American Art,
Smithsonian Institution, Washington D.C. USA*: 33. *University of Alabama/W.S. Hoole Special Collection Library*:
34. *The Museum of Mobile*: 37. *Alabama Department of Archives and History*: 42. *Erik Overby Collection,
University of South Alabama Archives*:45. *Archive Photos*: 50,97, 128 (right), 129, 131; Freddie Patterson, 87;
Joseph A. Rosen, 90; American Stock, 92, 128 (left); Sporting News, 95; Museum of the City of New York,
127; Popperfest, 132; Frank Driggs Collection, 134. *Alabama Music Hall of Fame*: 88. *Selma Chamber of
Commerce*: Mike Climmer, 72.

Printed in Italy

1   3   5   6   4   2

CONTENTS

ALABAMA IS . . .

Alabama is a place of beautiful land and friendly people . . .

"Alabama, your beautiful highways
Are carved through the mountains
Where loved ones do wait.
Alabama, your goldenrod flowers
And the welcome home sign
Hanging over the gate."
—from the song "Alabama," by Ira and Charlie Louvin

. . . and it is a place of racial division and conflict.

"Segregation now. Segregation tomorrow. Segregation forever."
—Governor George Wallace, 1963

Alabama is a place where tradition rules and time stands still . . .

"The present generation of people who had lived side by side for years and years, were utterly predictable to one another: they took for granted attitudes, character shadings, even gestures, as having been repeated by each generation and refined by time."
—from *To Kill a Mockingbird*, by Harper Lee

. . . but it is also a place that looks toward the future.

"When you look at Birmingham or Montgomery or Huntsville, you're looking at the future of the new South. You can see it everywhere; young people throughout our state are starting up their own businesses—developing new industries, new technologies and new ways to communicate. It wasn't too long ago that many of these same young people would have been working in steel factories or mining for coal. Today, more and more people are looking to the future and to new ways of doing things."   —business owner in Huntsville

Alabama is a place to leave . . .

"Frankly, I just couldn't stay there any longer. It finally got to where all people could see or could talk about was the color of the other person's skin. It broke my heart to leave Alabama, but I had just had enough of the hatred and the name-calling."

—retired schoolteacher who left Alabama
during the civil rights conflicts of the 1960s

. . . and a place to long for and return to.

"Sweet home, Alabama,
Lord, I'm comin' home to you."

—from the song "Sweet Home Alabama,"
by Edward King and Gary Rossington

Alabama is a land of suffering and strength, of internal conflict and startling creativity. Throughout its history, the state has been crippled by poverty, illiteracy, and racism. Over the years, however, Alabama's citizens have shown a stubborn determination to fight social injustice, to overcome personal adversity, and to create meaning and beauty out of hardship and struggle. Today, Alabamans—both black and white—are working to resolve the differences that have divided them in the past and to build their future together.

1 FROM MOUNTAIN TO SHORE

"**W**hen you talk about land, Alabama is really two or three different states rolled into one," explains a family physician in Gadsden. "As you travel across the state, you'll have a hard time getting people to agree about what Alabama is really like." Indeed, Alabama is a small but diverse state, with a wonderful array of natural landscapes.

NORTH ALABAMA

North Alabama forms the southernmost extreme of the Appalachian Mountains, the great mountain range that stretches diagonally across the eastern United States. The northeast is a region of sandstone ridges, deep green valleys, and the high, winding hills of the Beaver Creek Mountains. Over the years, mining companies searching for sandstone and limestone have blasted away the sides of ridges and hills in the area. This has left behind massive red clay walls rising where entire hills once stood. Today, these abandoned quarries are like giant wounds in the earth.

Farther west is an area of flatlands and gentle, rolling hills. Sometimes these hills empty suddenly into deep ravines cut by the region's many rivers and streams. In Winston County, in the northwest, stands Natural Bridge, the longest natural rock archway east of the Rocky Mountains. The enormous sandstone and iron ore

The highest point in the state, Cheaha Mountain rises to an elevation of 2,407 feet, almost half a mile high.

bridge spans 148 feet from one end to the other. The walkway is 33 feet wide and 8 feet thick. Atop the bridge are the remains of a fossilized tree that are at least four million years old.

North Alabama's most distinctive feature—even more than the rolling hills and steep cliffs of the Appalachian Mountains—is its plentiful water. The entire area is dotted with rivers, streams, lakes, and waterfalls. At the center of it all is the majestic Tennessee River. The sprawling waters of the Tennessee wind their way westward across much of north Alabama before twisting suddenly north to cut across the state of Tennessee. Alabama has dammed the river at several of its bends to form large reservoirs and recreational lakes. These include Lake Guntersville, Wheeler Lake, and Wilson Lake. The state has no natural lakes.

The Tennessee's countless tributaries have twisted and carved their way through the rock hills and limestone cliffs of northeast Alabama to form an impressive network of caves, natural springs, and waterfalls. These include DeSoto Falls, a spectacular one-hundred-foot waterfall near Fort Payne. The elaborate system of caves known as DeSoto Caves is the site of a two-thousand-year-old Indian burial ground. The caves were discovered in 1540 by explorer Hernando de Soto and were mined during the Civil War for minerals for making gunpowder. During Prohibition, when the nation outlawed the sale of liquor, bootleggers stored homemade liquor, called moonshine, in DeSoto Caves.

SOUTH ALABAMA

In contrast to the rolling hills and hardwood forests of north Alabama, south Alabama is covered primarily by flat, expansive meadows and farmlands and dense pine forests. Much of the area belongs to the East Gulf Coastal Plain. This region of beaches, marshland, and sandy clay soil spreads north from the Gulf of Mexico toward the center of the state. A wide band of dark, sticky clay, known as the Black Belt, stretches east and west across the coastal plain. The Black Belt has the

Natural creeks and springs wind their way through the caves and rocky hills of northeast Alabama. The one-hundred-foot drop of DeSoto Falls, near Fort Payne, is one of the more spectacular sights in the area.

state's most productive farmland. Large cotton farms once dominated the region.

Just south of the Black Belt, in the state's southwest corner, dark soil has formed between the banks of the Mobile and Tensaw Rivers. Known as the delta, this long, fertile stretch of land was formed over thousands of years, as regular flooding deposited rich mud from the bottom of the rivers in thick layers along the shore.

Moving through the delta toward the city of Mobile and the gulf coast, the land becomes spotted with marshes, bayous, and

SAVING THE ESTUARIES

When freshwater from rivers mixes with saltwater from the sea, you get estuaries. Estuaries and the marshy areas around them are home to abundant plant and animal life, including many species that can survive only in such mixed-water environments.

Some of Alabama's most interesting—and endangered—species make their homes in the sprawling estuaries near Mobile Bay. Salt marsh aster, sea lavender, and other beautiful plants grow in dense clusters in the sandy areas near Mobile Bay. In the swampy woods farther inland, flowers such as swamp cyrilla, black titi, and large gallberry bloom beneath the dark shade of water oaks and laurel oaks. Bald eagles soar undisturbed above the trees, while Florida black bears, marsh rabbits, eastern indigo snakes, and bayou gray squirrels roam through the woods. Beneath the dark estuary waters are gulf sturgeons, alligators, snapping turtles, and extremely rare Alabama shovelnose sturgeons.

In recent years, chemicals from factories have polluted Alabama's estuaries, while lumbering and land development have destroyed many inland swamps and forests. This has threatened the very survival of many plants and animals that need a mixed-water environment. In 1995, Alabama joined the National Estuary Program in an effort to preserve the large estuary at Mobile Bay. Restrictions were placed on draining swamps, cutting forests, and releasing chemicals into the environment. While it's too early to tell how much these changes have helped, Alabama enters the twenty-first century with a strong commitment to protecting these fragile environments.

In the southwest corner of the state, streams and rivers empty into vast marshes and bayous.

swamps. These shallow, tree-filled waterways are formed when rivers overflow and flood low inland fields. Many of them remain submerged in water year-round. "Kids growing up down here love to pretend they're living in the jungle," explains a store owner in Mobile. "The tangle of tall reeds, ferns, and vines along the swamps are sometimes so thick you really do need a machete to cut your way through, and even the shallowest waters are home to water moccasins [snakes] and snapping turtles and alligators. It really can be an adventure just making your way along."

Farther south, the deep green swamplands recede into the white sandy beaches that line Mobile Bay and the Gulf Shore. In the pale blue waters of the Gulf of Mexico, just west of the Alabama coast, two long, narrow islands—Pleasure Island and Dauphin Island—are the only remnants of a peninsula that once extended the mainland's sandy beaches into the gulf.

South Alabama has a rich supply of rivers, all flowing south toward the Gulf of Mexico. The largest are the Tombigbee, Alabama, Mobile, Tensaw, and Chattahoochee. As with the Tennessee River in the north, rivers in south Alabama have been dammed to form lakes. These include Lake Eufaula and the Walter F. George Reservoir on the Chattahoochee River, and Dannelly Reservoir on the Alabama River.

HOT AND STICKY

"It's just plain hot down here in Alabama," drawls a farm equipment supplier in Selma, using a handkerchief to wipe the perspiration from his forehead, "just plain out hot and humid all summer long. Ask anybody you want and they'll tell you the same

The white, sandy beaches of Alabama's gulf coast are among the most beautiful in the South.

thing. Don't come to Alabama if you don't like the hot, scorching weather. And if you don't like to sweat."

Alabama has a subtropical climate, which means it has short, mild winters and long, hot, humid summers. There is little if any snowfall during the winter, except in the northern hills. Low temperatures in the winter are frequently well above freezing. And in

LAND AND WATER

Pickwick Lake

Florence

Tennessee R.

Wilson Lake

Wheeler Lake

Huntsville

Tennessee R.

Decatur

Russellville

Guntersville Lake

Fort Payne

William B. Bankhead National Forest

Guntersville

Albertville

Weiss Lake

Cullman

Hamilton

Gadsden

Piedmont

Lewis Smith Lake

Talladega

Coosa R.

Anniston

Jasper

Locust Fork

Tallapoosa R.

Bankhead Lake

Birmingham

National Forest

Cheaha Mtn. (2,405 ft.)

Lake Tuscaloosa

Bessemer

Sylacauga

R.L. Harris Reservoir

Tuscaloosa

Lay Lake

Black Warrior R.

Talladega

Alexander City

Mitchell Lake

Coosa R.

National

Clanton

Lake Martin

Auburn

Lake Harding

Forest

Tombigbee R.

Lake Demopolis

Phenix City

Demopolis

Selma

Tallapoosa R.

Montgomery

William 'Bill' Dannelly Res.

Eufaula

Alabama R.

Greenville

Troy

Monroeville

Pea R.

Tombigbee R.

Choctawhatchee R.

Conecuh R.

Enterprise

Dothan

Chattahoochee R.

Andalusia

Brewton

Conecuh National Forest

Prichard

Mobile

Mobile Bay

	1,500 – 3,000 ft.
	600 – 1,500 ft.
	300 – 600 ft.
	0 – 300 ft.

0 10 20 30 40 50 60 70

MILES

the summer, the thermometer often reaches one hundred degrees. In her novel, *To Kill a Mockingbird*, Alabama native Harper Lee describes a typical summer day in the state during her childhood in the 1930s. "A black dog suffered on a summer's day," wrote Lee. "Men's stiff collars wilted by nine in the morning. Ladies bathed before noon, after three o'clock naps, and by nightfall were like soft teacakes with frosting of sweat and sweet talcum."

People in Alabama have developed their own ways to deal with the oppressive heat, which usually lasts for six or seven months each year. On the hottest summer days, men and women walk with a lazy, peaceful pace that seems almost like a slow-motion version of life in other parts of the country. In the early afternoons, farmers, construction workers, and other physical laborers pause frequently under the shade of oak and hickory trees to refresh themselves with ice water and share tales in slow, steady drawls.

A favorite toy of Alabama children during the summer is the common garden hose. One child will hold the end of the hose toward the sky, pressing her thumb lightly across the top of the nozzle to produce a wide spray of water that reaches from the grass all the way to the roof of the house. Friends then take turns running barefoot back and forth through the cool, refreshing mist, giggling and stomping their feet in the puddles that accumulate in the yard. On the sunniest days, the steady arc of water produced by the hose sometimes leaves a tiny rainbow shimmering across the yard.

Fierce thunderstorms and long steady rains are common in the summer. The average annual rainfall for Alabama's coastal regions is sixty-five inches, with fifty-three inches falling each year in the rest of the state.

A group of friends finds relief from the blistering summer heat at a popular swimming hole in Fish River.

PLANTS AND ANIMALS

Trees cover more than two-thirds of Alabama. The hills and valleys of north Alabama are colored by both the deep green leaves of hardwood trees, such as hickory and tall oaks, and the lighter green needles of softwood pines. The meadows and ridges of the coastal plain are dominated by the loblolly, short-leaf, and long-leaf southern pine.

The swamps and marshlands of the Mobile-Tensaw Delta and the gulf coast are filled with cypresses, cedars, magnolias, live oaks, and water oaks. Thick drapes of Spanish moss often hang from the massive limbs of the thick, squatty oak trees.

Thick clumps of Spanish moss drape the live oaks of southwest Alabama.

In the spring, brilliant crimson-colored azaleas brighten the southern half of the state. Along with the state flower, the camellia, Alabama's highways and back roads are dotted with the dazzling colors of goldenrods, asters, pinks, Dutchman's-breeches, orchids, and southern camasses.

The state's broad meadows, dense forests, and calm shores are filled with a rich variety of animals, including foxes, white-tailed deer, minks, skunks, bobcats, squirrels, rabbits, and raccoons. Beavers can frequently be seen building enormous wooden dams at the edges of riverbanks and lakes, and throughout the thick marshland of the Mobile-Tensaw Delta. Alligators are common in the swamps and bayous of southwest Alabama.

The state's many birds include bluebirds, cardinals, blue jays, and mockingbirds. The state bird, the yellowhammer, is a colorful member of the woodpecker family. The bird was named for the way it flashes the yellow underside of its wings as it hammers furiously against the tree bark with its beak. During the Civil War, Confederate soldiers adopted the bird as a mascot because its yellow and gray feathers matched the color of their uniforms. Hoping it would bring them luck, soldiers from Alabama wore the bird's feathers in their hats as they marched into battle.

With its extensive waters, Alabama also abounds in fish. Catfish, crappies, bream, drum fish, bull fish, and largemouth bass are common. The calm waters of Mobile Bay and the Gulf of Mexico are filled with a rich supply of fish and other forms of sea life, including flounder, mullet, red snappers, oysters, crabs, and shrimp.

With Alabama's vast supply of wildlife, hunting and fishing are popular. Across the state, hunters leave their homes before sunrise

JUBILEE

Each year between June and September, folks south of Mobile take part in the state's strangest traditional fishing activity. For generations, people from Spanish Fort, Daphne, and Fairhope have gathered each day on the eastern shore of Mobile Bay, wading barefoot in the shallow waters for an event known as Jubilee. They come to the beach to await the arrival of great teams of fish, crabs, and shrimp that are rumored to be drawn mysteriously to the site during the summer.

According to legend, the fish and crustaceans arrive each year en masse and quickly become disoriented by the shallow waters and the waves bursting on the shore. For a brief period, the animals float helplessly in the backwash from the waves, and many of them wash up on shore. No one knows for sure which day the swarms of sea creatures will arrive. But local residents who are lucky enough to pick the right day to patrol the shore simply help themselves to all the fish, crabs, and shrimp that they can carry away with them in the buckets and ice chests that they brought from home.

on weekend mornings to track ducks, rabbits, white-tailed deer, quail, and the state's most popular game bird, the wild turkey. Wild turkeys are among the most difficult animals to track and hunt. For one thing, the fleet-footed birds are shy and reclusive. Hunters are forced to wander into remote areas of the forest to find the birds' roosting places. Wild turkeys also blend well with the natural colors in the woods and can easily scamper to safety beneath thickets and brush.

In the 1940s, wild turkeys were hunted with such frequency that they almost disappeared from Alabama. Since that time, the state

Alligators are common in the swamps and bayous of southwest Alabama.

Upper right: The deep, calm waters of Mobile Bay and the Gulf of Mexico are the home for a wide variety of marine life, including ghost crabs.

Black bears and a host of other wild animals prowl the dense forests and broad meadows across the state.

Almost extinct in the 1940s, Alabama's state bird, the wild turkey, can now be found in abundance throughout the state.

has created special wildlife sanctuaries to protect the bird. Today, Alabama once again boasts one of the largest populations of wild turkeys in the nation. In certain areas, the birds can often be seen in small groups, wobbling nonchalantly along the roadside.

"The wild turkey is a lot like Alabama," explains a man near Muscle Shoals. "It's not the fastest or the strongest bird in the

woods, and it's certainly not the flashiest. But it's a proud bird and determined to survive. Try sneaking up on one. You think you're about to take it by surprise, and, all of a sudden, it's ducked into a hollow or scampered through the brush. It's gone, just like that."

2 STRUGGLE AND CHANGE

Tennessee River, Alabama, *by unidentified artist*

"You can say what you want to about Alabama," says an African-American teacher from Mobile, "but we're determined and resourceful people. There have been a lot of rough spots in our history, a lot of things that none of us are particularly proud of. There are all types of people here—black and white, city and country—and we haven't always seen eye to eye on things. But no matter how big the differences have been between us, and no matter how tough things have gotten, we've always found a way to make something better of our lives. That history of struggle and change is really what our state is all about."

FIRST INHABITANTS

People began living in what is now Alabama about 12,000 years ago. At first, they lived in small groups, supporting themselves by hunting, fishing, and gathering fruits and vegetables that grew in the wild. In winter they found shelter in such places as Russell Cave, first occupied more than nine thousand years ago. Eventually, some began to settle in larger, more permanent communities. They cleared the land and grew their own vegetables and fruits. Around these larger settlements emerged the different Indian nations who would later greet—and often struggle against—the region's earliest

In this painting by George Catlin, Choctaw Indians play a ballgame similar to lacrosse.

European settlers. In Alabama, these nations included the Creeks, Cherokees, Choctaws, Alabamas, and Chickasaws.

At Moundville Archaeological Park in central Alabama, visitors can walk through the South's largest example of a permanent Native American settlement. The Indians who originally lived there lugged heavy bags of dirt on their backs for long distances to build towering mounds on which they made homes for their leaders and burial grounds. From these mounds, the Indians had a clear view of the nearby Black Warrior River and other areas from which enemies might arrive. Today, the park preserves twenty-six of these mounds.

EUROPEANS ARRIVE

The first Europeans to reach present-day Alabama were led by the Spanish explorer Alonso Álvarez de Piñeda, who sailed into Mobile

Armed with only bows, arrows, and tomahawks, Chief Tuskalusa and his men were no match for De Soto's armed horsemen.

Bay in 1519. In 1528, another Spanish expedition sailed through Alabama's coastal waters without going ashore.

Twelve years later, Spaniard Hernando de Soto became the first European to explore the state's interior. De Soto and his troops entered Alabama in the northeast and then marched and rafted southward down its entire length. On their journey, they met with Native Americans and traded supplies with them. The Indians were outraged, however, when de Soto enslaved some Indians to serve as guides and to carry his troops' supplies.

When de Soto and his men reached the village of Mabila, just north of present-day Mobile, the Indians fought back. But Chief Tuskalusa and his Choctaw warriors were outnumbered by de Soto and his troops. And their bows, arrows, and tomahawks were of little use against the Spaniards' muskets. After their victory, de Soto's men burned the Indian village to the ground before continuing to the gulf.

CHANGING FLAGS

More than 150 years would pass before the first permanent European settlement was established in Alabama. In 1702, two French-Canadian brothers, Pierre Le Moyne, Sieur d'Iberville, and Jean Baptiste Le Moyne, Sieur de Bienville, founded a settlement called Fort Louis on the banks of the Mobile River. In 1711, the river flooded, destroying the city. The French moved their settlement twenty-seven miles downriver to the site of present-day Mobile. This city served as the capital of French Louisiana until 1722, when New Orleans was chosen for the honor.

In the coming years, the European powers fought over the area that included Alabama. When the American colonies gained their independence from England in 1783, northern Alabama became part of the United States, while southern Alabama remained in the hands of the Spanish. In 1795, the United States acquired most of Alabama from Spain. Only the gulf coast and the area around Mobile remained under Spanish rule.

Then, in the nineteenth century, the United States and Spain fought a number of costly battles over the gulf coast region held by

POPULATION GROWTH: 1800–2000

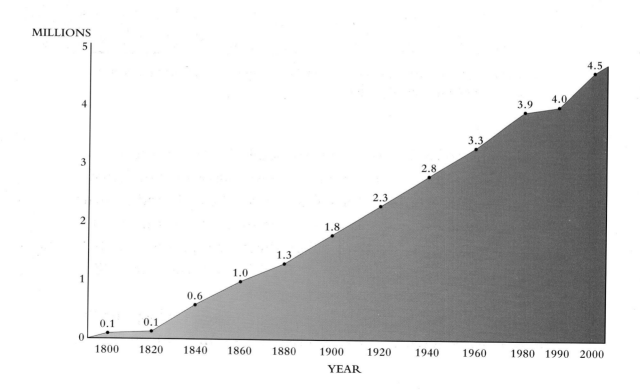

The port city of Mobile was home to both French and Spanish settlers before it was acquired by the United States.

the Spanish, and a U.S. fleet captured Mobile. With guns and ammunition supplied by the Spanish, many Native Americans also declared war on the United States. They were angry at being forced off their land as the United States expanded its territory westward. In 1813, a large army of Creeks attacked Fort Mims, near present-day Tensaw. The Creek warriors captured and burned the fort, killing hundreds of American soldiers in the process.

Despite this defeat, U.S. troops eventually prevailed against the united forces of the Spanish and the Creeks. In 1814, American forces led by General Andrew Jackson decisively defeated Creek warriors and their half-English chief, William Weatherford, in the Battle of Horseshoe Bend. Both the Spanish and the Creeks surrendered all of their land west of the Coosa River to the United States.

Other Native American tribes—including the Choctaws, Cherokees, and Chickasaws—continued to live in scattered pockets throughout the region until 1838, when federal troops forced them from their homes into territories farther west. Thousands of Native Americans died from cold and disease during the difficult journey west.

EARLY STATEHOOD

In 1819, Alabama became the twenty-second state admitted to the Union. During the early years of statehood, wealthy cotton planters from the Carolinas and Georgia began settling in Alabama. With the help of thousands of African slaves, they cleared the land and built large plantations in the fertile Black Belt and Tennessee Valley.

Their dreams of establishing a new cotton empire were shattered, however, when a series of droughts devastated many of the state's cotton farms. The young state faced one crisis after another. A nationwide depression that began in 1837 led Governor Benjamin Fitzpatrick to shut down the state bank in 1843 without repaying people who had money in the bank. Many wealthy farmers and businesspeople were suddenly left penniless. Then an epidemic of yellow fever killed hundreds of people across Alabama.

No one in Alabama suffered more during this period than slaves. By the 1850s, almost one out of every two Alabamans was a slave.

The majority worked on plantations and small farms, where they picked cotton by hand from sunrise to sundown. It was back-breaking labor, leaving the men, women, and children who worked the fields with sore bodies and bleeding fingers at the end of each day.

THE CIVIL WAR

As the nineteenth century progressed, more and more Northerners began to condemn the practice of slavery. They wanted to outlaw slavery throughout the nation. The Alabama Platform, adopted by the state Democratic convention in 1848, argued that each state had the right to determine whether its citizens could own slaves. In the years that followed, the arguments between Northerners and Southerners over the issues of slavery and states' rights became ever louder.

At the 1860 Democratic convention, Alabaman William Lowndes Yancey campaigned for the passage of the Alabama Platform by the national party. When the convention refused to adopt the Alabama Platform, Yancey led the entire state delegation back to Alabama and out of the national Democratic Party. The refusal of Alabama and other Southern states to support the Democratic candidate in the presidential election of 1860 was a major factor in the election of Republican Abraham Lincoln. The new president supported a strong federal government and opposed slavery.

On January 11, 1861, Alabama officially withdrew from the Union, declaring itself the independent Republic of Alabama. Less than a month later, Alabama joined with its Southern neighbors to

MOBILE BAY

In the nineteenth century, cotton was king in Alabama. Much of this cotton left the state at Mobile. In 1861, the year the Civil War began, slaves loaded a million bales of cotton onto ships in Mobile Bay. It is from them that we get this variation of a sailor's song.

pump a-way.   John-ny come tell us and pump a-way.   pump a-way.

And how many bales can you carry on?
Johnny come up and tell us and pump away.
Just hurry up before she's gone.
Johnny come and tell us and pump away. *Chorus*

The times are hard and the wages low,
Johnny come and tell us and pump away.
Just one more bale before we go,
Johnny come and tell us and pump away. *Chorus*

If ever good luck does come my way,
Johnny come and tell us and pump away.
I'll say goodbye to Mobile Bay,
Johnny come and tell us and pump away. *Chorus*

An outspoken defender of slavery, William Lowndes Yancey led an angry group of Alabama delegates out of the national Democratic convention in 1860.

form the Confederate States of America. Montgomery, the largest city in the Black Belt, was chosen as the Confederacy's capital.

Vowing to preserve the Union at all costs, President Lincoln sent Union soldiers to naval ports throughout the South. On April 12, 1861, the Civil War began. The most important battle in Alabama was at Mobile Bay in 1864, when Union admiral David G. Farragut soundly defeated the Confederate forces. "Damn the torpedoes! Full speed ahead!" Farragut shouted to his crew as his ship was being attacked. When the Confederacy finally surrendered after four years of war, much of the South was in ruins.

In the decades following the war, Alabama prospered. While cotton farming thrived in the Black Belt, mining and iron production blossomed in the central and northern parts of the state. Hundreds of mines sprang up in northern Alabama to unearth the region's iron and charcoal. Soon, Birmingham became one of the world's great iron and steel centers.

Admiral David G. Farragut led Union forces during the Battle of Mobile Bay in 1864.

THE LEGEND OF HENRY WELLS

On a stormy night in the small town of Carrollton, children crowd nervously around the courthouse to catch a glimpse of one of Alabama's strangest attractions. According to local legend, the image of former slave Henry Wells appears momentarily on one of the courthouse's second-story windows each time a lightning bolt fills the night sky with light.

As the story goes, a raging fire destroyed Carrollton's original courthouse in 1876. Wells was suspected of committing the crime, but he escaped the area. Two years later, Wells was arrested in another part of the state and brought back to Carrollton for trial. As the news spread that Wells had been captured, an angry crowd gathered outside the recently rebuilt courthouse.

In the decades following the Civil War, African Americans accused of serious crimes were often lynched, or hanged without a trial. To protect Wells from the mob, authorities secretly moved him to a guarded room on the second floor. While a powerful thunderstorm settled over the area, Wells watched the angry crowd with terror, his face pressed against the second-story windowpane. All at once, a bolt of lightning crashed down on the street below, momentarily scattering the crowd. According to legend, the sudden burst of bright light permanently engraved Wells's image on the window. Wells was later killed while attempting to escape, but the image of his face remains a vital legend in Carrollton.

THE DEPRESSION AND THE TVA

Alabama's newfound prosperity suffered a number of setbacks during the early twentieth century. During the 1920s and 1930s, a tiny insect called the boll weevil invaded the state's cotton fields by the millions.

During the Great Depression of the 1920s and 1930s, thousands of Alabama's citizens lived in poverty. In Mobile and other cities, poor blacks often lived in dilapidated wooden villages known as shantytowns.

Entire crops were quickly destroyed. Many farmers were left in financial ruin. During the same period, the Great Depression swept across the nation and the world. Between 1929 and 1931, most banks in Alabama were forced to close, leaving depositors without their money. Tens of thousands of Alabamans lost their jobs.

Alabama's future did not brighten until the federal government created the Tennessee Valley Authority (TVA) in 1933. The TVA's purpose was to control flooding and create cheap electric power.

TUSKEGEE

In the late nineteenth century, an educator named Booker T. Washington was responsible for one of the most significant events in Alabama history. The son of a Virginia slave family, Washington used money he received from foundations and philanthropists to establish the Tuskegee Institute, founded in 1881 in the small town of Tuskegee, Alabama. Washington believed that education was the key to the liberation of black people in the United States. Students at the school worked the farmland around Tuskegee at the same time that they studied agricultural sciences and other courses. Washington eventually transformed the small experimental school into the nation's most respected black educational institution.

In 1896, Washington hired a brilliant young African-American scientist named George Washington Carver to teach at the institute. Carver was already respected for his research in botany, the study of plants, and mycology, the study of mushrooms and other fungi. During the decades he taught at Tuskegee, Carver became one of the world's leading botanists and one of the nation's leading educators. His specialty was finding creative uses for common plants and vegetables. His most famous discoveries involved the peanuts that grew in abundance in the rich Black Belt soil around Tuskegee. Over the years, Carver and his students created 325 products from the peanut, including peanut butter.

Government workers quickly built two new dams on the Tennessee River and restored a third. During the same period, the newly formed Alabama Power Company also began to dam rivers and build power plants. With the inexpensive electricity supplied by these new plants, Alabama's iron and steel factories began to hum once again, providing jobs for thousands of unemployed people. Others found jobs clearing the land and building the dams. "That TVA was a godsend for the people of this state," recalls a retired schoolteacher in Huntsville. "All of a sudden, folks were up and working again, supporting their families and building up the state."

THE CIVIL RIGHTS MOVEMENT

But Alabama's renewed prosperity was not for everyone. The nearly one million African Americans who lived there continued to suffer under the "Jim Crow" laws, which had existed since the decades following the Civil War. Under this system of racial segregation, or separation, black Alabamans were not allowed to enroll at the same schools, hold the same positions, or use the same water fountains, bathrooms, or other public facilities as white Alabamans. But this began to change in 1954, when the U.S. Supreme Court declared racial segregation in public schools unconstitutional. Inspired by the Court's historic decision, many African Americans in Alabama began to struggle openly for their rights.

Things heated up the following year, when a woman in Montgomery named Rosa Parks refused to surrender her bus seat to a white man. At the time, blacks in Alabama and throughout the South were required by law to sit in the back of public buses. And

In 1955, Montgomery native Rosa Parks was arrested for refusing to give up her seat on a city bus to a white man. "I had decided that I would have to know once and for all what rights I had as a human being and a citizen," she later recalled.

if the whites-only section became full, black riders had to give up their seats in the back to white riders.

Parks had always felt that segregated seating was unfair. She had often tried to take a seat closer to the front of the bus, but each time she had failed. On several occasions, drivers had asked her to leave the bus. "Our treatment was just not right," Parks would later say, "and I was tired of it. I kept thinking about my mother and my grandparents, and how strong they were. I knew there was a possibility of being mistreated, but an opportunity was being given to me to do what I had asked of others."

When Parks refused to leave the bus, she was arrested and brought to trial for breaking Montgomery's racial-segregation laws. Outraged by her treatment, Dr. Martin Luther King Jr., who was then a local minister at Dexter Avenue Baptist Church, and others organized a boycott of the citywide Montgomery bus system. To protest Parks's arrest, African Americans began walking and carpooling to and from work each day instead of riding the bus. Since nearly half of Montgomery's citizens were African American, the boycott, which lasted more than a year, devastated the city's transportation system. In November 1956, the U.S. Supreme Court finally ended the case by declaring that segregated seating in public transportation was unconstitutional.

But this did not end the public conflict over civil rights in Alabama. A key figure would be the state's outspoken governor, George Corley Wallace. In 1958, Wallace began his campaign for governor as a progressive Democrat who supported greater rights for blacks and other poor Alabamans. After he was soundly defeated by a racist white candidate, Wallace changed his stance on racial issues. As a vocal supporter of segregation, he was elected to four terms as governor during the next three decades.

In 1963, Wallace brought international attention to the state when he stood defiantly at the doorway of Foster Auditorium at the University of Alabama and refused to allow black students to enroll at the school. In response, President John F. Kennedy sent in the National Guard, and the students were eventually allowed to attend. However, Wallace's bold stance made him the spokesperson for white people who supported segregation. "Governor Wallace knew how to get people fired up," remembers a librarian in Mont-

One of the state's most colorful public figures, Governor George Wallace (left) was a stubborn supporter of racial segregation during the 1960s.

gomery. "He knew exactly how white Alabamans were reacting and feeling to the changes that were happening around us." In 1968, 1972, and 1976 Wallace ran for president, first as an independent candidate and then as a Democrat. Though he was not elected, he received millions of votes across the country.

CONTINUING THE STRUGGLE

In recent years, black and white Alabamans have begun to work together to improve their state and to protect the rights of all its citizens. Surprisingly, a leader in the state's new style of politics was George Wallace himself. During his final campaign for governor in 1982, Wallace completely changed his position on racial issues, speaking out on behalf of the rights and needs of the state's black citizens. He even received an outpouring of black support during the election. Wallace began to focus Alabama politics on issues such as health care, public education, and creating new jobs that would benefit all the state's citizens.

During the past decade, black and white Alabamans have struggled to continue to improve the quality of life in their state. "We've got a hard road ahead of us," says a Mobile teacher. "Black people and white people in Alabama have spent so much time pointing fingers at one another and blaming each other for everything that's wrong about the state. But we're finally beginning to see how much more we can get done if we stop accusing one another and start working together. I think our best days are ahead of us."

3 WORKING TOGETHER

The state capitol in Montgomery

Each state has its own form of government and its own style of making and changing laws. Like many southern states, Alabama has a conservative, slow-moving government. In order for changes to occur, Alabama's citizens have sometimes had to speak out against and publicly defy the old laws—sometimes at great personal risk. In fact, many of the most significant changes in the state's history—such as the civil rights legislation of the 1950s and 1960s—have only happened in response to the widespread protests of Alabama citizens.

In spite of these dramatic events, politics plays a relatively minor role in the thoughts and lives of the majority of Alabamans. "We in Alabama aren't really very political as people," explains a real estate agent in Auburn. "Sure, we feel strongly about issues here in Alabama; we just don't tend to think of everything in political terms. Instead we like to deal with important issues on a smaller scale and in more personal terms."

INSIDE GOVERNMENT

Alabama's government is divided into three branches: executive, legislative, and judicial.

Executive. The chief executive of Alabama is the governor. He or she prepares the state budget and develops policies in areas ranging

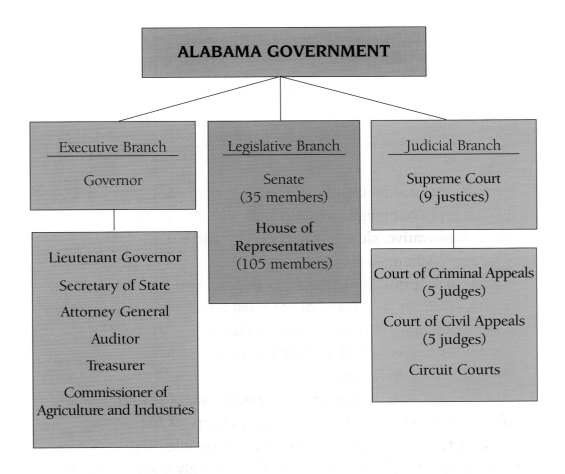

ALABAMA GOVERNMENT

Executive Branch

Governor

Lieutenant Governor

Secretary of State

Attorney General

Auditor

Treasurer

Commissioner of
Agriculture and Industries

Legislative Branch

Senate
(35 members)

House of
Representatives
(105 members)

Judicial Branch

Supreme Court
(9 justices)

Court of Criminal Appeals
(5 judges)

Court of Civil Appeals
(5 judges)

Circuit Courts

from education to economic development. The governor, who is chosen every four years, may serve no more than two consecutive terms. The same is true for the lieutenant governor, who takes over if the governor must leave office during the term. This happened in 1993, when Governor Guy Hunt was replaced by Lieutenant Governor James Folsom after being convicted of ethics violations.

Other executive branch officials include the attorney general, the state auditor, the secretary of state, the state treasurer, and the commissioner of agriculture and industries.

Legislative. The Alabama legislature consists of a senate with 35 members and a house of representatives with 105 members. All legislators are elected to four-year terms. The legislature is responsible for approving budgets and drafting and approving new legislation. After the legislature approves a proposed law, called a bill, it is sent to the governor to be signed. If the governor signs the bill, it becomes a law. If the governor vetoes, or rejects, the bill, it can still become law if it is repassed by a majority of members in both the senate and the house.

Judicial. Alabama's highest court is the state supreme court. It is composed of a chief justice and eight associate judges, who are elected to six-year terms.

Most of Alabama's criminal and civil trials are heard in the circuit courts. If someone challenges a decision made in a circuit court, the case is heard by either the court of criminal appeals or the court of civil appeals, each of which has five judges. If the ruling of the appellate court is also challenged, the case is then sent to the state supreme court for a hearing.

THE HARD ROAD TO CHANGE

The most important political issue in Alabama during the last century has been the division between the races. But the question of civil rights has always been much more than a political issue for the people of the state. The struggle for racial equality goes to the heart of basic values such as fairness, pride, and the dignity of each individual.

In March 1965, Martin Luther King Jr. led protesters on a fifty-

In 1965, thousands of citizens marched fifty miles from Selma to the capitol steps in Montgomery to protest racial injustice in the state.

mile march from the Black Belt city of Selma to the capitol steps in Montgomery. Many of the 3,200 marchers were terrified as they joined arms to cross the bridge leading out of Selma. They had reason to be afraid. Police on horseback had charged into the group and used tear gas when they had tried to begin the march two weeks earlier. And several people had been beaten during the days that followed. "To tell you the truth, I wasn't sure that I wanted to get involved in that mess," admits a woman who was eight years old when she took part in the march. "I was fearful that something bad would happen, with people being beaten and attacked the weeks before we left. But as afraid as I was, I still wanted to be in the midst of things and to be involved somehow. You just had to have a certain faith and determination and commitment that what you were doing was right. That's what brought us together, and that's what kept us going through it all."

By the time the protesters reached the capitol, their number had swelled to more than 25,000. The national attention given to the march helped gather support for the Voting Rights Act of 1965, which guaranteed voting rights to all Americans.

MAKING A LIVING

During Alabama's early history, its economy was built around cotton farming and textile production. For more than a century, most Alabamans, both black and white, made their living in the cotton fields or working in some part of the cotton textile industry. But after the boll weevil destroyed thousands of acres of cotton in the early twentieth century, people began to look for more reliable ways to make a living.

Many of Alabama's cotton farms were converted to other crops. Today, there are still 45,000 farms in Alabama. Most are relatively small, averaging only about two hundred acres apiece. Three-fourths of Alabama's farmlands are devoted to raising livestock, such as chickens and cattle. The remaining one-fourth is devoted to crops, including cotton, hay, soybeans, and vegetables. Peanuts are also grown in abundance.

Before the boll weevil arrived in the early twentieth century, most people in Alabama made their living planting and harvesting cotton. Today, cotton pickers still work fields across the state's Black Belt region.

With more and more of Alabama's people moving out of small farming communities and into cities and towns, service industries have become increasingly important to the state's economy. "When I was a child," recalls an accountant from Cullman, "most people either worked in a factory somewhere or lived on a farm. Nowa-

SAUSAGE CHEESE GRIT CASSEROLE

In Alabama and throughout the South, grits (the popular name for ground hominy corn) are both a favorite breakfast food and a key ingredient in many dinner casseroles. Have an adult help you with this recipe.

6 cups water
1½ cups quick grits
2 tablespoons unsalted butter
2 large pickled jalapeño chiles (finely minced)
4 scallions (finely chopped)
2½ cups shredded cheddar or Monterey jack cheese
¾ pound fresh sausage
1 tablespoon vegetable oil
1 onion (finely chopped)
1 large red or green bell pepper (finely chopped)
4 large eggs
2 teaspoons hot sauce

In a large saucepan, bring the water to a boil and slowly stir in the grits. Cover and simmer, stirring occasionally, for 7 minutes. Stir in the butter, the minced jalapeño, the chopped scallions, and 1½ cups of cheese. Add salt and pepper to taste. Stir until the cheese is melted and then spread the mixture in a buttered 9-by-13-inch baking dish.

Brown the sausage over medium heat in a heavy skillet, stirring frequently and breaking the lumps. Use a slotted spoon to transfer the sausage to a paper towel to dry. Pour the fat from the skillet, and then add oil. Cook the chopped onion and bell pepper over medium heat, stirring until both are soft. Whisk together the eggs and hot sauce in a bowl, adding salt to taste. Stir in both the sausage and the onions-peppers, and then spread the entire mixture over the grits. Finally, sprinkle the remaining cheese over the top.

Bake in an oven preheated to 350 degrees until the eggs are firm, about 30 minutes. Serve hot.

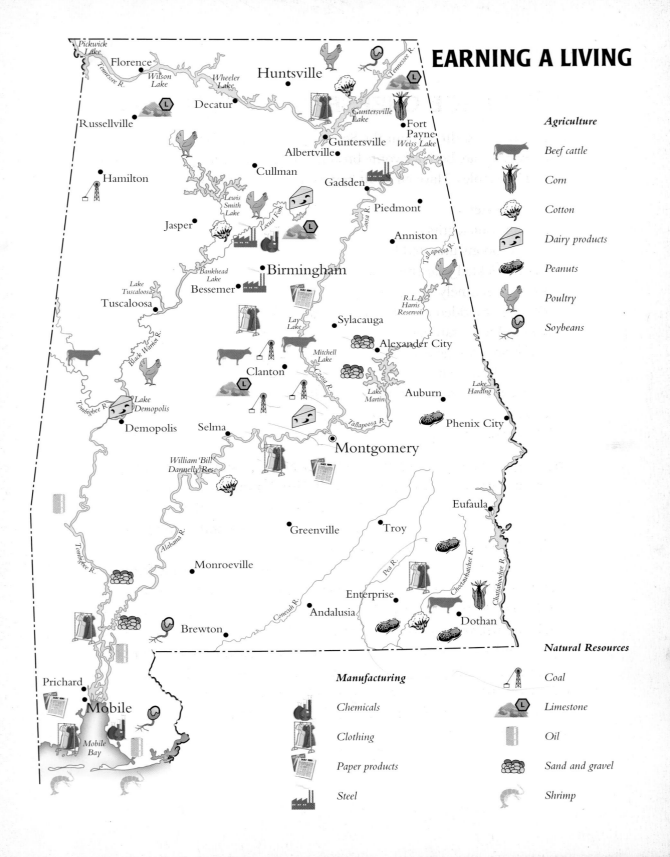

EARNING A LIVING

Agriculture

- Beef cattle
- Corn
- Cotton
- Dairy products
- Peanuts
- Poultry
- Soybeans

Manufacturing

- Chemicals
- Clothing
- Paper products
- Steel

Natural Resources

- Coal
- Limestone
- Oil
- Sand and gravel
- Shrimp

Pickwick Lake
Florence
Wilson Lake
Wheeler Lake
Huntsville
Tennessee R.
Guntersville Lake
Decatur
Russellville
Guntersville
Fort Payne
Weiss Lake
Albertville
Hamilton
Cullman
Gadsden
Lewis Smith Lake
Piedmont
Coosa R.
Jasper
Locust Fork
Anniston
Tallapoosa R.
Birmingham
Bankhead Lake
Lake Tuscaloosa
Bessemer
R.L. Harris Reservoir
Tuscaloosa
Black Warrior R.
Lay Lake
Sylacauga
Alexander City
Mitchell Lake
Clanton
Auburn
Lake Harding
Tombigbee R.
Lake Demopolis
Coosa R.
Lake Martin
Demopolis
Selma
Tallapoosa R.
Montgomery
Phenix City
William 'Bill' Dannelly Res.
Eufaula
Alabama R.
Greenville
Troy
Monroeville
Pea R.
Chattahoochee R.
Tombigbee R.
Choctawhatchee R.
Enterprise
Conecuh R.
Andalusia
Dothan
Brewton
Prichard
Mobile
Mobile Bay

GROSS STATE PRODUCT: $80 BILLION

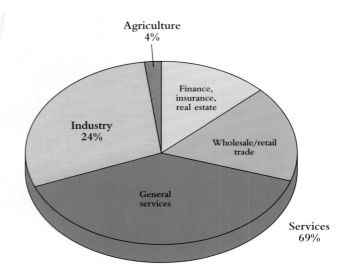

Agriculture
4%

Finance,
insurance,
real estate

Industry
24%

Wholesale/retail
trade

General
services

Services
69%

(2000 estimated)

days, it seems like everybody you know is in the city, working for the government or the schools or some type of public service. Now, most people put on a suit and tie to go to work, and they drive there in their nice new car. I don't think that younger people realize how different things used to be, just a generation ago." Today, service industries account for roughly 70 percent of the gross state product.

The state's largest service industries are supported by the government. Alabama's largest employer is the public school system. The army and air force bases that are located across the state are also important to Alabama's economy. The George C. Marshall Space Flight Center in Huntsville, one of the largest research facilities of the National Aeronautics and Space Administration (NASA), is also a major employer. The Saturn V rocket that carried the first astronauts to the moon was designed and tested at the center.

Paper mills and other factories throughout the state operate using electricity provided by Wilson Dam and other power plants located among the sprawling lakes of north Alabama.

The state's rich mineral supply and cheap electricity have made it one of the South's centers of manufacturing. Paper, clothing, transportation equipment, and iron and steel are all produced in Alabama. Most of the state's iron and steel plants are in Birmingham and Bessemer.

Mining is another important sector of the Alabama economy.

When you think of Birmingham, you just naturally think of iron and steel, says a local resident with pride. Since the nineteenth century, Birmingham and nearby Bessemer have served as one of the nation's centers of iron and steel production.

Huge limestone quarries are scattered across the state's northeast corner, and coal mines can be found throughout north-central Alabama. Natural gas and petroleum are drilled near Mobile.

Other sources of income in Alabama include forestry—primarily growing yellow pine trees—and fishing. Shrimp is the state's leading seafood. Catfish are also farmed in lakes and ponds across the state.

EDUCATION

Historically, many Alabamans have suffered from poor education. The Alabama legislature did not create a statewide public education system until 1854, thirty-five years after statehood was declared. Even after public schools were established, poor children worked in the fields most of the year. The children of slaves received no schooling at all.

Thousands of Alabama's citizens are employed harvesting and preparing wood from the state's dense forests of yellow pine trees. Here, a trainload of freshly cut wood chips stretches along the railroad tracks.

After slavery ended, black children and white children were educated in separate schools, and far more money was spent on the schools for white children. Consequently, black children received a poorer education. Not until schools began to be desegregated in the 1960s did equal education become available to black children.

In the 1980s, Governor George Wallace began pushing to improve education. He helped pass a $310 million statewide

Since the 1980s, Alabama has taken dramatic steps to improve education for students in public schools throughout the state.

bond that has been responsible for dramatic improvements in the quality of Alabama's public schools. Since then, Alabama has made education a priority. One important step has been to adopt strict standards for core courses. Public high school students must now complete four years of English, social studies, science, and mathematics. "In the past decade, Alabama has significantly raised the bar for what we expect," says one Montgomery teacher. "We now have the most rigorous graduation requirements of any state in the nation. We still have a long way to go to make things right for our students, but I feel confident that we're finally headed in the right direction."

4 THE HEART OF DIXIE

With Tennessee to the north, Georgia to the east, Mississippi to the west, and Florida to the south, Alabama is literally the geographical center of the Deep South. Alabamans have traditionally prided themselves in being more truly southern than anyone else. "They don't call us the Heart of Dixie for nothing," says a highway patrolman from Selma. "You can't get any deeper into the South than Alabama."

BLACK AND WHITE

For most people in Alabama, being southern means sharing a common history and a common way of life. But while the lives of most black and white Alabamans have been shaped by the same past and the same dramatic events, they often have very different memories of their shared history.

In recent years, one issue dividing black and white residents has been the continued use of the Confederate flag across the state. Many white Alabamans still choose to demonstrate their southern pride by displaying the Confederate flag on T-shirts, caps, and bumper stickers or draped across the rear windows of pickup trucks. "I'm a southerner," explains a customer at a gas station in

In spite of its controversial history, the Confederate flag is still a symbol of southern pride for many white Alabamans.

Huntsville with a picture of the Confederate flag on his cap, "and the flag has always stood for the South. It's just as simple as that."

For many black Alabamans, however, the display of the Confederate flag is a sore spot. "It's just so insensitive to keep using it," complains a store owner in Mobile, "and you still see it everywhere you go. I know that lots of people don't mean any harm by it, but to me, that flag represents a time and a way of life when my ancestors were slaves. So of course it upsets me every time I see it."

Today, in spite of their differences, black and white Alabamans are increasingly finding ways to share the memories and symbols of

At an outdoor class in Selma, students learn about the struggles and sacrifices that have brought the people of their state together.

their state's past. Throughout the year, thousands of black and white citizens visit shrines to and re-creations of the two most dramatic and significant events in the state's troubled history: the Civil War and the civil rights movement.

Visitors to Selma can learn about both of these. Each April, actors re-create the 1865 Battle of Selma, the state's only major inland Civil

War battle. In the struggle for the Confederate army's largest iron foundry, the Union forces defeated Confederate troops led by General Nathan Bedford Forrest. Forrest would later become famous as the first leader of the Ku Klux Klan, a white supremacist organization that became powerful after the war.

Across town at the National Voting Rights Museum and Institute, the same visitors can learn about the civil rights march from Selma to Montgomery one hundred years after the Battle of Selma. "It's just amazing to think about all the important things that happened here in Selma," says an African-American mother who visited the city with her two small children. "And to see black children and white children coming here like this and learning

ETHNIC ALABAMA

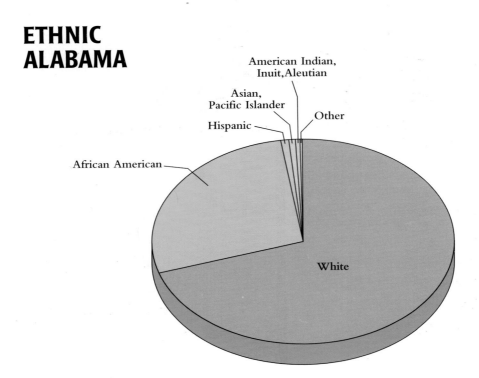

about their city together—and their parents here with them—it gives me so much hope for the future."

Throughout the year, Alabamans also celebrate their southern heritage through a remarkable number of school and family homecomings and local festivals. Each spring, cities and towns across the

The National Voting Rights Museum and Institute in Selma is filled with memories and symbols of the struggle for racial equality in Alabama.

At the annual spring festival in Mobile, women dressed in pre-Civil War clothing stroll among the flowering dogwoods, azaleas, and magnolias.

state hold elaborate pilgrimages in which neighborhoods open their oldest and most beautiful homes to visitors. The most popular spring pilgrimages take place in Selma and Eufaula. Visitors come from all over to see the azaleas, dogwoods, and magnolias in full

THE RATTLESNAKE RODEO

Each March, the tiny town of Opp is host to one of Alabama's strangest and most entertaining festivals. More than 40,000 people crowd into the town stadium to eat cotton candy, hear live country music, and watch one of the world's largest rattlesnake rodeos.

Visitors can purchase wallets and hats made from rattlesnake skin, and key chains and earrings made from rattles. Children can learn the proper techniques for "milking" a rattlesnake (draining the venom from its fangs) and treating snakebites. There's also plenty of fried rattlesnake for everyone to eat, as well as a special ceremony in which a local elementary school girl is crowned Little Miss Rattlesnake Rodeo Princess.

The highlight of the event is the rattlesnake race, in which a barrel full of diamondback rattlers is dumped in the middle of a chalk circle. The first snake to wriggle its way outside the circle is the winner, and the race is often completed in a matter of seconds. The big thrill is watching the rattlesnake handlers as they try to round up all the snakes before they can reach the stands full of screaming onlookers. In the words of one spectator, "The snakes down here are a really good reason to consider wearing cowboy boots."

bloom and to tour the beautiful pre–Civil War mansions. Other popular Alabama festivals celebrating the state's southern heritage include Winfield's Mule Day, Syrup Soppin' Days in Loachapoka, and Selma's Tale Tellin' Festival, where colorful ghost stores are a favorite among local children.

CHURCH

Alabama lies near the center of the region known as the Bible Belt. Most Alabamans are members of conservative Protestant denominations, where revival meetings are commonplace and the Bible is the principal authority for making decisions. Baptists account for more than half of the state's churchgoers. Methodists, making up a little more than 10 percent, are the next largest group, followed by Roman Catholics, at slightly more than 4 percent.

Each Sunday morning the state's roads are heavy with traffic, as families drive to their local churches. In hundreds of small towns throughout the state, the steeples and spires that rise above Protestant churches are often the tallest and the most beautiful sights on the horizon. In addition to the large Protestant denominations, many Alabama churchgoers belong to small independent churches. Driving through some of Alabama's rural communities, motorists pass by one congregation after another with names like Independent Baptist Church, Holiness Baptist Church, Separate Baptist Church, and Foot Washing Baptist Church.

Alabamans are typically very proud of—and very vocal about—their religious beliefs. Many believe that it is extremely important to share their religious beliefs and values with other people. "We here in

Most Alabamans are faithful churchgoers. Local worshippers leave the Sunday morning service at St. Andrew's Episcopal Church in Prairieville.

Alabama quite often don't agree about what we believe," explains a Methodist minister from Mobile, "but most of us feel strongly that our beliefs should make a difference in our lives, both in our families and personal relationships and throughout society as a whole. Sometimes we also feel it's necessary to speak out publicly about what we believe and make ourselves heard, even if the things we have to say aren't popular or well received at the time."

Throughout the state's history, Alabamans have frequently taken public positions based on their religious beliefs. In the 1950s, Dr. Martin Luther King Jr. used his pulpit at Dexter Avenue Baptist Church to condemn the racial segregation that was practiced at the time. In recent years, Protestants in Alabama have spoken out in support of a number of causes, often involving the rights of citizens to express their religious beliefs in public settings, such as public schools and workplaces. In 1997, more than six thousand conservative Alabamans gathered in Montgomery to show their support for Etowah County judge Roy Moore.

For years, Judge Moore had begun his court sessions with a public prayer. He also kept a reproduction of the Ten Commandments on the wall of his judge's chamber. Earlier in the year, an Alabama circuit judge had ordered Judge Moore to remove the Ten Commandments from his chamber and to stop using prayer in his courtroom. The federal court ruled that, as a public servant, the judge did not have the right to express his private religious beliefs in the courtroom. The court's ruling was based on "the separation of church and state," a legal doctrine that ensures that both the government and religious institutions can operate independent of one another's control. When Judge Moore refused to comply with the court's ruling, conservative Christians, including the governor, rallied in Montgomery to express their dissatisfaction with the court's decision.

"Sometimes you have to be willing to stand up and be counted," said one of the protestors. "We believe that every person in this state should have the right to practice his religious beliefs, whenever and wherever he pleases. I don't think the courts have any sense at all just how important our religious beliefs are to us down here. That's why we came together as a group—to say to the courts and the federal government once and for all, 'Enough is enough. It's time you listened to what we have to say.'"

In 1998, Judge Moore and his supporters won a temporary victory when the state supreme court dismissed the case, thereby avoiding making a ruling. In the meantime, Alabamans continue to disagree—and to express their disagreement—over the proper relationship between religion and politics.

SPORTS

Sports play an enormous role in the lives of Alabamans. Everywhere you go in the state, there are signs of some type of sporting event—from sprawling green golf courses and soccer fields to huge football stadiums and the speedway in Talladega.

When most people in Alabama talk about sports, the first thing they mention is football—especially the fierce contest between the state's two powerhouses, the University of Alabama and Auburn University. From the waterways of northwest Alabama to the sandy shores of Mobile, virtually everyone in the state has something to say about the rivalry. "Sports are almost like a religion here in Alabama," confides a student at Auburn, "especially football. Sometimes things get a little crazy in the fall, especially when it comes to the Auburn-Alabama rivalry. I've actually seen family members who wouldn't even speak to each other during the weekend of the game, because each one was rooting for a different team. During the football season, just about everybody in the state is either an Alabama fan or an Auburn fan. It's just not something you can be neutral about."

With their records over the years, the two teams have certainly given Alabamans plenty to talk about. One of the most successful teams in the history of college football, Alabama has won twelve national titles during the past seventy-five years. Some of the game's most talented and popular athletes—including quarterbacks Bart Starr and Joe Namath—first received national attention while playing at Alabama.

Alabamans of all ages are passionate about sports.

But it was the team's legendary coach, Paul "Bear" Bryant, who captured the imagination and respect of the people of Alabama. Bryant led the University of Alabama to six national championships and became the most successful coach in college football history, with 323 wins overall. Even Alabama's rivals at Auburn are in awe of Bryant's accomplishments and respectful of his memory.

In recent years, however, Auburn has begun to challenge Alabama's dominance as the state's best team. During the 1970s and 1980s, two of the team's outstanding players—quarterback Pat Sullivan and running back Bo Jackson—received the Heisman Trophy as the year's best college football player.

The second most popular sport in Alabama is stock-car racing. Located east of Birmingham, the Talladega Superspeedway hosts some of the world's fastest stock cars. The shelves and bedsides of youngsters throughout the state support model race cars and photographs of top drivers. Each October, racing fans from around the country crowd into the speedway to watch the Winston 500. "For my money and my time," says an automobile mechanic in Auburn, "there's nothing in this world that's more exciting than car racing. You've got the speed and the roar of the tires and all that energy among the crowd. There's just absolutely nowhere I'd rather be than up there at Talladega. Nowhere."

Some of the world's fastest stock cars race on the Talladega Superspeedway.

5 ALABAMA ALL-STARS

When it comes to Alabamans who have made their mark on the nation, music and sports are king. But many Alabamans have also made important contributions in public service, literature, and other fields.

THE KING OF COUNTRY MUSIC

Country music legend Hiram "Hank" Williams was born in 1923, near the small town of Georgiana. Hank first learned about music as a three-year-old sitting beside his mother, who played the organ in the local Baptist church. When he was twelve, Hank became friends with an African-American street musician named Rufus Payne, who was nicknamed Tee-Tot. Payne earned nickels and dimes playing for anyone who would listen on the quiet streets of Georgiana. He taught Hank how to play guitar, sing, and capture the attention of a live audience.

By age thirteen, Hank had formed his first band, the Drifting Cowboys. Though the actual musicians would change, the name of the band would remain the same throughout his career. During his teens, Hank matured into the most gifted singer and songwriter in the history of country music. But he also developed a serious drinking problem and a habit of getting into trouble on and off the stage.

Known as the King of Country Music, Hank Williams lived only twenty-nine years but wrote and recorded some of the most popular songs in the history of American music.

In 1948, when he was only twenty-four, Hank got his first taste of fame when he recorded the spirited tune "Lovesick Blues." Within a few months, the song had sold three million copies. Soon, Hank reigned as the undisputed King of Country Music, recording a string of classic songs including "Hey, Good Lookin'," "Take These Chains from My Heart," and "Your Cheatin' Heart."

Sadly, at the same time his songs were rising to the top of the charts, Hank's personal life was in a shambles. His marriage ended in divorce, and his hard drinking continued to damage both his health and the quality of his live performances. On January 1, 1953,

Hank was found dead of a heart attack in the back seat of his Cadillac. In his hand, he clutched a piece of paper on which he had just written the lines to a new song: "We met. We lived and, dear, we loved. Then comes that fatal day; the love that felt so dear fades far away." At the time of his death, Hank Williams was just twenty-nine years old.

THE LOUVIN BROTHERS

If Hank Williams was country music's most celebrated singer and songwriter, the Louvin Brothers set the standard by which all coun-

"Our mother used to sing us these old ballads," said Charlie Louvin of the traditional songs on which he and his brother Ira staked their reputation. "A lot of people that we were raised up in Alabama with were lovers of folk music."

try duets are measured. Ira and Charlie Louvin grew up in the rural community of Sand Mountain in the 1930s. From their earliest childhood, their lives were filled with traditional music. At night on the radio they listened to the leading folk music acts of the day, such as Bill Monroe and the Delmore Brothers. They also learned about music by listening to their family and neighbors, who would crowd into each other's homes every few nights to serenade one another with folk ballads and gospel hymns.

Early in their career, the Louvin Brothers were strictly a gospel duet. The cover to their album *Satan Is Real* showed Charlie and Ira singing in front of the flames of hell, with the devil himself standing in the background. In 1955, the brothers finally released their first nongospel single, the ballad "When I Stop Dreaming." The song quickly became a hit.

The following year, the Louvin Brothers released their masterpiece, the country album *Tragic Songs of Life*. It was a perfect blend of traditional tunes, mournful romantic ballads, and patriotic anthems. All the songs were delivered with the clean, tight harmonies that made the Louvin Brothers' music so heartbreakingly memorable. Many people still regard it as the finest country duet ever recorded. Charlie and Ira never re-created this success, but their music continues to influence country singing.

AN INSPIRING LIFE

In the 1880s in the small town of Tuscumbia, a child not even two years old fell ill with a high fever. By the time the fever had passed, she had lost both her sight and her hearing. She was completely cut

SUN RA

Even as a teenager, Herman "Sonny" Blount was clearly different from everyone else. When not practicing piano, he would walk around Birmingham dressed like a monk, his feet bare and a long white robe draped across his shoulders. But if Sonny's behavior was a little strange, he was also a brilliant musician. He was a standout both in his high school jazz band and with several professional jazz combos.

After he graduated from high school, Sonny moved to Chicago. There he spent countless hours studying the music of big band leaders like Duke Ellington. He also began to read mystical literature, such as the Egyptian Book of the Dead and books on astrology. Influenced by these books, Sonny changed his name to Sun Ra, after the Egyptian sun god. He began telling people that he was a messenger from the planet Saturn. He claimed he had been sent to Earth to bring peace and harmony through a new form of mystical music. He also formed his own big band, which he called the Astro-Intergalactic-Infinity Arkestra, to help him share his new music with the world.

Over the years, Sun Ra's beliefs and behavior became more and more offbeat. He wore outrageous costumes, including bright robes, enormous necklaces, and tall, oddly shaped hats. Eventually he moved to New York City, where he became one of the most influential figures in twentieth-century experimental music. Along the way, Sun Ra introduced a number of important elements to big band music, including electronic instruments, drama and dance, and jazz improvisation.

off from the outside world, unable to communicate her needs or feelings with anyone.

But this girl, whose name was Helen Keller, was very determined, and she struggled to reach out to the people in her life. Each day she would clutch her mother's skirt and follow her around the house and farm. Eventually, Helen began to recognize people and places by the way they smelled and felt. She also learned to do routine tasks, such as making bread and milking cows. She even developed her own sign language, using physical gestures to communicate her needs to her family.

Helen's life really began to change when Anne Sullivan was hired to take care of her. Sullivan was a brilliant teacher of Braille, a special alphabet that uses raised dots on the page, so that sightless people can use their fingertips to read. Sullivan was certain that she could teach Helen to read and to speak. At first, Helen resisted Sullivan's efforts. She threw violent tantrums whenever the young woman approached her.

But one day, as Sullivan pumped the iron handle on the old family well, Helen held her hand beneath the cool stream of water. Seeing an opportunity, Sullivan took one of Helen's hands away from the water and pressed it to her lips. She repeated the letters W-A-T-E-R over and over again as she continued to pump from the well. All at once, Helen understood the connection between the movements of Sullivan's lips and the cool liquid that she felt rushing through her fingers. Helen was thrilled by her new discovery. She led her teacher around the yard, touching familiar objects and then placing her fingers to Sullivan's mouth to feel the letters of each object's name repeated on her lips. Over time, Helen learned

Tuscumbia native Helen Keller (pictured here with her teacher, Anne Sullivan) overcame great adversity to become a world-famous writer and public speaker.

to read and write using Braille. She even learned to speak.

Sullivan eventually took her gifted young student to special schools in Boston and New York. Helen became an outstanding student. In 1904, at age twenty-four, she graduated from Radcliffe College, a prestigious college in Massachusetts for women. She then became a successful public speaker, giving lectures supporting women's rights and social and economic reform. She also founded the American Foundation for the Blind. Her autobiography, *The*

Story of My Life, continues to be an inspiration to people facing hardships and disabilities.

HAMMERIN' HANK

Throughout the 1950s and 1960s, two Alabama natives, Willie Mays and Henry "Hank" Aaron, competed with New York Yankee Mickey Mantle for the title of the game's greatest hitter. Most people believed that Mantle and Mays had the best chance of breaking Babe Ruth's legendary record of 714 career home runs. Both men impressed the fans with their towering home runs, their blinding speed on the bases, and their colorful style of play.

Mobile native Hank Aaron had always practiced a less flashy, but more consistent, playing style. While Mays made diving catches in center field, Aaron rarely moved more than a few feet to catch the ball. He never had to. He studied the batters' records so thoroughly that he usually knew exactly where the ball would go before it was hit. Even before the ball left the bat, Aaron was already standing at the precise spot in right field where it would land. And instead of the lofty home runs produced by Mantle and Mays, Aaron hit hard, low line drives to all corners of the field. Many of Aaron's home runs barely cleared the wall.

"I came to the Braves on business," Aaron would later say of his no-nonsense style, "and I intended to see that business was good as long as I could." Aaron continued to play in the same businesslike style for more than twenty years with the Milwaukee Braves, the Atlanta Braves, and the Milwaukee Brewers. Throughout his career he averaged thirty-three home runs and almost one hundred runs batted in per season. When Mays and Mantle began to slow down in the late 1960s, Aaron continued to produce at the same steady pace. Finally, on April 8, 1974, he slapped a fastball into the bleachers. It was his 715th career home run, sending him past Babe Ruth as baseball's all-time home run leader. By the time he retired in 1976, Aaron had amassed 755 home runs, a record that still stands.

OLD SATCH

One of the greatest baseball players to call Alabama—or any other state—home had little chance to display his talents before major league fans. Leroy Robert "Satchel" Paige was born in 1906, on the south side of Mobile. A tall, lanky youngster whose arms reached all the way down to his knees, Satchel could hurl a baseball past professional athletes when he was still in high school.

During the 1920s and 1930s, Paige became the dominant pitcher in the Negro Leagues. At the time, African-American athletes were not allowed to compete in the Major Leagues. Instead, the most gifted black players banded together to form their own leagues. Paige, who often pitched on consecutive days, led his teams to several championships.

Throughout most of his career, he played baseball year-round. During the off-season, he and other players formed informal teams and went "barnstorming." They drove around the country competing against the most talented players in each town where they stopped. Several times, Satchel and his barnstorming teammates competed against groups of all-stars from the white Major Leagues.

Growing up in Mobile in the 1920s, pitching sensation Satchel Paige heard the same message from southern baseball scouts again and again: "We sure could use you, if you were only white."

Most of the time, the Negro League players got the best of their white opponents. White Hall of Fame pitcher Dizzy Dean once drawled, "That skinny old Satchel Paige, with those big arms, is my idea of the best pitcher with the greatest stuff I ever saw."

In 1947, Jackie Robinson joined the Brooklyn Dodgers to become the Major Leagues' first African-American player. The next year, at age forty-one, Satchel Paige made his Major League debut with the Cleveland Indians. "Twenty-two years," Paige complained about the years he had waited for his chance, "is a long time to wait to be a rookie."

Paige was already past his prime by this time. He spent just four and a half years in the Majors. In 1965, Paige pitched in the Majors for the last time, as a publicity stunt for the Kansas City Athletics. Incredibly, the fifty-nine-year-old legend pitched three shutout innings against the powerful Boston Red Sox. The only hit he allowed was a double to Red Sox slugger Carl Yastrzemski.

All told, Satchel Paige won more than two thousand games during his forty-five years of barnstorming and league play. Many of the game's greatest players—including Dean, Joe DiMaggio, and Ted Williams—considered him the greatest pitcher of all time.

WRITERS

One of the twentieth century's most gifted writers, Truman Capote, was born in New Orleans, Louisiana, in 1924. His parents divorced when he was young, and he was sent to live with relatives in the small Alabama town of Monroeville. During his years in Alabama, Truman became close friends with a local girl named Harper Lee. Years later, Lee would achieve fame by writing *To Kill a Mockingbird*, a moving story about race relations in a small southern town. Lee would model one of the main characters in the story, a boy named Dill, on her childhood friend Truman.

After Truman's mother remarried, the family moved to New York City. By the time he entered high school, he had already demonstrated his skills as a writer, and he was soon sending his short stories to prestigious magazines. His first novel, *Other Voices, Other Rooms*, was published when he was only twenty-four. Ten years later, his novel *Breakfast at Tiffany's* made him famous. The book was made into a popular motion picture, with actress Audrey Hepburn starring as the charming heroine. In the early 1960s, Capote and his childhood friend Harper Lee traveled across Kansas, investigating a gruesome murder that had taken place a few years earlier. Capote wrote a powerful book called *In Cold Blood* about the crime. Although Capote never returned to Alabama to live, in such works as his classic story "A Christmas Memory," he returned there often.

The distinguished novelist Truman Capote celebrated the memories of his childhood in Alabama in the short story "A Christmas Memory."

6 OUT AND ABOUT IN ALABAMA

From Mobile to Birmingham to Huntsville, each of Alabama's cities and towns provides a different picture of life in the state and a unique expression of Alabama's colorful history and culture.

HUNTSVILLE

Huntsville, the biggest city in north Alabama, is known primarily as the home of the U.S. Space & Rocket Center. Along with an original Apollo rocket, which was designed in Huntsville, the museum also displays the space shuttle *Pathfinder* and a full-size Saturn V rocket.

Across town, Huntsville offers a glimpse into the past at the Alabama Constitution Village, where the state's first constitution was signed in 1819. More than a dozen buildings have been rebuilt or restored to represent the time, including a carpenter's shop and a post office. Men and women dressed in clothing from the period demonstrate how people used to make quilts, spin thread, and build furniture.

Southeast of Huntsville, Lake Guntersville State Park is one of Alabama's most spectacular woodland areas. The park's six thousand acres are filled with natural wonders. Bluebirds, nesting eagles, and beavers building dams are common sights, and visitors frequently stumble across the trees and shrubs where wild turkeys roost.

One of the state's most spectacular sights, Lake Guntersville abounds in herons, eagles, bluebirds, and other colorful wildlife.

THE SHOALS

West of Huntsville, the cities of Muscle Shoals, Tuscumbia, Sheffield, and Florence are scattered across both banks of the Tennessee River. To Alabamans, the entire area is known simply as the Shoals. The region's most spectacular sight is the majestic Tennessee River, along with its lakes and tributaries. "If you ask me," says a truck driver near Florence, "this is the most beautiful part of Alabama, with the big open skies and the light dancing off the river. Sometimes the sun sets so brightly on the water that I can barely see to drive."

Near Florence, Wilson Dam has one of the world's largest single-lane water locks. The lock is a deep concrete passageway that can be filled with water to allow boats or barges to pass from one section of the river to the other. Walkways along the lock allow visitors to watch as boats slowly pass by.

TEN LARGEST CITIES

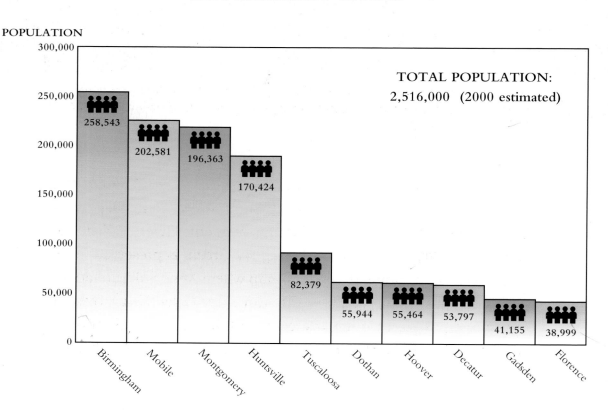

POPULATION

TOTAL POPULATION: 2,516,000 (2000 estimated)

City	Population
Birmingham	258,543
Mobile	202,581
Montgomery	196,363
Huntsville	170,424
Tuscaloosa	82,379
Dothan	55,944
Hoover	55,464
Decatur	53,797
Gadsden	41,155
Florence	38,999

A carefully preserved memorial at Ivy Green, Helen Keller's childhood home in Tuscumbia, includes the original water pump where Anne Sullivan taught Keller her first word.

The Shoals is also famous for its music. W. C. Handy, the composer known as the Father of the Blues, was born in a log cabin in Florence. The Shoals' most famous resident, Helen Keller, was born in Tuscumbia. The Keller home, Ivy Green, is preserved in its original form, including the water pump where Anne Sullivan taught Keller her first word. Each June, the three-day Helen Keller Festival features a parade through the center of Tuscumbia and several performances of *The Miracle Worker,* a play about Keller's early life.

THE FATHER OF THE BLUES

"Where the Tennessee River, like a silver snake, winds her way through the red clay hills of Alabama," wrote William Christopher Handy in his autobiography, "sits high on these hills my hometown, Florence. I was born in a log cabin which my grandfather had built." Today the original log cabin in which Handy was born is preserved in Florence. A nearby museum includes the piano on which he composed many of his songs and the golden trumpet that he played on stage.

Handy first heard the blues while traveling through the Mississippi Delta in 1903. He immediately fell in love with the music. In the following years, Handy began to incorporate the odd rhythms and mournful lyrics of the blues into many of his compositions, such as "The St. Louis Blues" and "The Memphis Blues." During the early decades of the twentieth century, his songs first brought the blues, gospel, and other African-American musical forms to an international audience.

BIRMINGHAM

Located in north-central Alabama, Birmingham is the industrial, scientific, and cultural center of the state. It is Alabama's largest city and one of the great cities of the Deep South. In the late nineteenth century, Birmingham became one of the country's leading steel producers. The city grew so fast that it was nicknamed the Magic City. During the twentieth century, the city's economy had expanded to include finance, education, engineering, and medical technology.

But Birmingham still bears the marks of its heyday as a city of steel. The most spectacular example of Birmingham's steel-producing past is the Sloss Furnaces National Historic Landmark. Though the furnaces shut down in 1971, the plant's massive iron-works and towering blackened smokestacks still stand.

Another popular Birmingham site is the Alabama Sports Hall of Fame. Among its many treasures are the game ball from the

Towering above the evening sky, the massive smokestacks of the Sloss Furnaces National Historic Landmark recall the heyday of iron and steel production in Birmingham.

University of Alabama's legendary football coach Paul "Bear" Bryant's record-breaking 315th victory and the Heisman Trophy won by Auburn University quarterback Pat Sullivan. Additional exhibits celebrate the careers of other popular Alabama sports heroes, including Willie Mays, Henry Aaron, Jesse Owens, Joe Louis, Bobby Allison, and Bart Starr.

Birmingham's most memorable sight, however, is the massive statue of the mythical god Vulcan that stands proudly atop Red Mountain in the southern part of the city. The statue was created as Birmingham's contribution to the 1904 world's fair in St. Louis, Missouri. Vulcan is the largest iron statue in the world and the second-largest statue of any type in the United States. Only the Statue of Liberty is larger. Visitors can either climb the steps or take an elevator to the top of Vulcan for a spectacular view of the city and the green rolling hills around it.

MONTGOMERY

The state capital of Montgomery is a startling combination of the Old South and the New South. An active business center, the city has become crowded with high-rise office buildings and hotels. But at the center of the city—in the shadow of the skyscrapers—Alabama's most enduring symbols of the pre–Civil War South can be found.

The state's huge white capitol building stands proudly above the city's downtown on a steep green hillside called Goat Hill. Erected in 1851, the building has a massive domed center, six three-story columns guarding the entrance, and an enormous clock

LOONEY'S TAVERN

Hidden away in the heart of the Bankhead National Forest in north Alabama's Winston County is one of the state's most interesting landmarks. A park and amphitheater mark the site of Looney's Tavern, the headquarters of pro-Union sympathizers during the Civil War.

In the years before the war, most farmers in north Alabama were relatively poor. Many of them opposed slavery, while others were unwilling to fight to protect a way of life that they could not afford themselves. Defying the new Confederate government, residents of the area established the "Free State of Winston," a slave-free community that continued to support the Union.

Bill Looney, popularly known as the Ol' Black Fox, led the movement from his tavern in the forest. During the Civil War, he personally guided more than 2,500 people through the woods to join Union troops in Decatur and Huntsville.

Today, locals proudly celebrate this odd, defiant chapter in Alabama history. Each summer, actors present *Legacy*, a drama about Bill Looney and the other citizens of the Free State of Winston. Visitors can also see a re-creation of Looney's Tavern and take a riverboat cruise.

perched atop the roof. Inside, two magnificent circular stairways wind their way to the third floor with no visible signs of support.

In 1861, the building served for a few months as the first capitol of the Confederate States of America. Confederate president Jefferson Davis took his oath of office on its front porch. He and his family lived briefly in the big white house that is now across Washington Avenue from the capitol. Today, the former presidential mansion contains an impressive collection of documents and

One of the more remarkable features of the capitol building in Montgomery is the magnificent spiral staircase that winds its way from the ground floor toward the ceiling three stories above.

artifacts from the Civil War period, including items that once belonged to Davis.

The Dexter Avenue King Memorial Baptist Church lies just one block down the hill from the capitol steps. In the mid-1950s, Dr. Martin Luther King Jr. served as the church's pastor, gathering support for the Montgomery bus boycott from its pulpit. Today a colorful mural in the church basement portrays the courageous people who took part in the boycott, as well as other important moments in the civil rights movement.

Russell Cave
National Monument

U.S. Space & Rocket Center

Pickwick
Lake

Florence

Wilson Dam

Alabama Constitution Village

Ivy
Green

Wilson
Lake

Wheeler
Lake

Huntsville

Lake Guntersville
State Park

Russellville

Decatur

Fort
Payne

DeSoto State Park

Sloss Furnaces National
Historic Landmark

Hamilton

Guntersville

Weiss Lake

Albertville

Cullman

Gadsden

Alabama Sports
Hall of Fame

Lewis
Smith
Lake

Piedmont

Statue of Vulcan

Jasper

Locust Fork

Coosa R.

Tallapoosa R.

Birmingham Zoo

Bankhead
Lake

Anniston

Lake
Tuscaloosa

Birmingham

▲ Cheaha Mtn.
(2,405 ft.)

Bessemer

R.L.
Harris
Reservoir

Tuscaloosa

Lay
Lake

Sylacauga

Alexander City

Black Warrior R.

Mitchell
Lake

Lake
Harding

Clanton

Coosa R.

Auburn

Phenix
City

Lake
Martin

Tombigbee R.

Lake
Demopolis

State Capitol

Demopolis

Selma

Dexter Avenue King
Memorial Baptist Church

Montgomery

Alabama R.

William 'Bill'
Dannelly Res.

Civil Rights Memorial

Eufaula

Greenville

Troy

Tombigbee R.

Monroeville

Pea R.

Choctawhatchee R.

Chattahoochee R.

Conecuh R.

Andalusia

Enterprise

Dothan

Brewton

Fort Condé

Bienville Square

Prichard

Mobile

Oakleigh Garden Historic District

Mobile
Bay

Gulf State Park

Bon Secour National Wildlife Refuge

U.S.S. Alabama Battleship Memorial Park

PLACES
TO SEE

Nearby is the Civil Rights Memorial. It was designed by the sculptor Maya Lin, who also created the Vietnam Veterans Memorial in Washington, D.C. It features a circular stone tablet bearing the names of people who sacrificed their lives for the civil rights movement. A steady stream of water washes across the surface of the stone. The wall behind the monument bears words from the Bible that King frequently quoted: "Until justice rolls down like waters and righteousness like a mighty stream."

Designed by celebrated architect Maya Lin, the Civil Rights Memorial in Montgomery features a stone tablet bearing the names of all those who sacrificed their lives during the civil rights movement.

MOBILE

Mobile is Alabama's second-largest city and only seaport. The site of the first permanent European settlement in Alabama, it is also one of the oldest cities in the South.

At the center of the city, Fort Condé, the site of the original French settlement almost three hundred years ago, has been restored. Inside the fort's thick walls are replicas of the cannons and muskets that the French used to conquer the region. In the nearby park Bienville Square, rows and rows of giant live oak trees stand close together, their huge branches heavily draped with Spanish moss. For several weeks each spring, the more than half a million azalea trees that fill the park and line the city streets paint Mobile in dazzling crimson.

Oakleigh Garden Historic District features some of the Deep South's most impressive homes from the 1800s. Oakleigh, one of the largest and most beautiful of these stately mansions, was built in the 1830s and has been carefully preserved. Locals still proudly describe how President James Garfield once sipped his first mint julip on the mansion's expansive front porch.

South of the city, Gulf State Park and the Bon Secour National Wildlife Refuge are two of the South's most popular recreational areas. The pure white sands of Gulf State Park are among the most beautiful beaches on the gulf coast. The wildlife refuge offers a rich array of beachside and wilderness trails, along which visitors can see pelicans, bobcats, and alligators.

In Mobile Bay, just west of the city, is the U.S.S. *Alabama* Battleship Memorial Park. The *Alabama* is an enormous ship that carried

MARDI GRAS IN MOBILE

While most people associate Mardi Gras with New Orleans, the festival has a longer history in Mobile. The first official Mardi Gras celebration in North America was held in Mobile in 1703, more than one hundred years before the event made its way to New Orleans. Mardi Gras was named for the days of feasting that took place just prior to Lent, a traditional time of self-sacrifice and fasting before Easter.

Today, thousands of people still line the streets to watch a parade of masked revelers and colorful floats. People on the floats toss candies, coins, and other souvenirs to children in the crowd. In the Mobile version of Mardi Gras, the most popular items to catch are moon pies, chocolate- or vanilla-coated graham cookies with a marshmallow center. All along the parade route, people stand with their arms outstretched, yelling "Moon pie! Moon pie!" at the top of their lungs and then leaping to catch the cookies.

Built in the 1830s, Oakleigh is among the largest and most beautiful of the stately homes that fill the garden district of Mobile.

2,500 crewmen into battle during World War II. Anchored nearby, the *Drum* is a submarine that was also used during World War II. Both vessels are open to the public, so visitors can climb up to the *Alabama*'s two-story observation deck and explore the long, creepy,

low-ceilinged hallways that wind through the narrow interior of the submarine.

"It's hard not to be moved by all the memories here in Mobile," says a visitor from Anniston. "It makes you think about all the things the people in our state have been through over the years.

A fighter plane growls at the U.S.S. Alabama in Mobile.

We've fought for change and for freedom again and again—against foreign rulers, against slavery, against laws that weren't fair. But somehow, we've always managed to preserve the things that were beautiful and true from our past. And I hope we always will."

THE FLAG: *The Alabama flag, which is based on the Confederate battle flag, shows a red cross against a white background. It was adopted in 1895.*

THE SEAL: *Adopted in 1819, the state seal bears a map of Alabama indicating the state's rivers, which were important to its economic development.*

STATE SURVEY

Statehood: December 14, 1819

Origin of Name: From the Alibamu Indians, whose name means "I clear the thicket."

Nickname: Heart of Dixie

Capital: Montgomery

Motto: We Dare Defend Our Rights

Bird: Yellowhammer

Flower: Camellia

Tree: Southern pine

Saltwater Fish: Tarpon

Mineral: Red iron ore

Rock: Marble

Camellia

ALABAMA

The Alabama legislature adopted this as the official state song on March 3, 1931.

Words by Julia S. Tutweiler   **Music by Edna G. Gussen**

Al - a - ba - ma, Al - a - ba - ma, we will aye be true to thee,

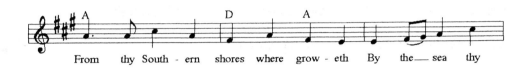

From thy South - ern shores where grow - eth By the sea thy

o - range tree. To thy North - ern vale where flow - eth

Deep and blue thy Ten - ne - see. Al - a - ba - ma,

Al - a - ba - ma, we will aye be true to thee.

Monarch butterfly

Horse: Racking horse

Freshwater Fish: Largemouth bass

Game Bird: Wild turkey

Insect: Monarch butterfly

Gemstone: Star blue quartz

GEOGRAPHY

Highest Point: 2,407 feet above sea level, at Cheaha Mountain

Lowest Point: sea level along the Gulf of Mexico

Area: 51,718 square miles

Greatest Distance, North to South: 329 miles

Greatest Distance, East to West: 210 miles

Bordering States: Mississippi to the west, Tennessee to the north, Georgia to the east, and Florida to the south

Hottest Recorded Temperature: 112°F in Centreville on September 5, 1925

Coldest Recorded Temperature: -27°F in New Market on January 30, 1966

Average Annual Precipitation: 56 inches

Major Rivers: Alabama, Black Warrior, Chattahoochee, Coosa, Mobile, Perdido, Tallapoosa, Tennessee, Tombigbee

Major Lakes: Eufaula, Guntersville, Martin, Pickwick, Weiss, Wheeler, Wilson

Trees: cedar, cypress, hemlock, hickory, oak, pine, poplar, sweet gum

Wild Plants: aster, azalea, dogwood, Dutchman's-breeches, goldenrod, mountain laurel, orchid, rhododendron

Animals: alligator, bobcat, deer, gray fox, mink, opossum, rabbit, raccoon, red fox, skunk

Red fox

Birds: cardinal, duck, flycatcher, goose, heron, mockingbird, osprey, swallow, whippoorwill, wild turkey

Fish: bass, bream, buffalo fish, catfish, crappie, garfish, flounder, mackerel, mullet, red snapper, tarpon

Endangered Animals: Alabama beach mouse, Alabama cavefish, Alabama cave shrimp, Alabama redbelly turtle, American peregrine falcon, Anthony's riversnail, black clubshell, boulder darter, cracking pearlymussel, gray bat, Gulf moccasinshell, Indiana bat, oval pigtoe, oyster mussel, pink mucket, red-cockaded woodpecker, tulotoma snail, West Indian manatee, wood stork

Wood storks

Endangered Plants: Alabama canebrake pitcher-plant, Alabama leather-flower, gentian pinkroot, green pitcher-plant, harperella, leafy prairie-clover, Morefield's leather-flower, pondberry, relict trillium, Tennessee yellow-eyed grass

TIMELINE

Alabama History

1400s Cherokee, Chickasaw, Choctaw, Creek, and other Indians live in present-day Alabama

1519 Spanish explorer Alonso Álvarez de Piñeda becomes the first European to see Alabama when he sails into Mobile Bay

1540 Spaniard Hernando de Soto leads the first European expedition into the interior of Alabama

1549 Tristán de Luna founds Alabama's first European settlement near present-day Claiborne, but it lasts just three years

1702 French Canadians found Fort Louis on the Mobile River

1711 Fort Louis is moved to present-day Mobile, becoming Alabama's first permanent European settlement

1783 At the end of the American Revolution, northern Alabama becomes U.S. territory

1795 Spain cedes most of present-day Alabama to the United States

1814 The Creek Indians give up their land in Alabama west of the Coosa River to the United States

1817 Alabama Territory is established

1819 Alabama becomes the 22nd state

1838 The U.S. government forces the Indians to leave Alabama and move west

1846 Montgomery becomes the state capital

1854 The state establishes a system of public schools

1861 Alabama secedes from the Union and joins the Confederate States of America; the Civil War begins

1864 The Union wins the Battle of Mobile Bay

1868 Alabama is readmitted to the Union

1881 Booker T. Washington organizes the Tuskegee Institute to educate African Americans

1888 Steel is first produced in Alabama

1890s Iron and steel manufacture becomes the state's leading industry

1901 The state's sixth and present constitution is adopted

1924 Construction is completed on Wilson Dam, the first dam on the Tennessee River

1933 The Tennessee Valley Authority is created to control flooding and provide cheap electricity

1941–1945 The United States engages in World War II

1955 Rosa Parks refuses to give up her seat to a white passenger on a segregated bus, setting off the Montgomery bus boycott

1963 Governor George Wallace tries to block the integration of the University of Alabama; four black girls are killed in the bombing of a Baptist church in Birmingham

1965 Martin Luther King Jr. leads a civil rights march from Selma to Montgomery

1986 Guy Hunt is elected the state's first Republican governor since the 1870s

Peaches

ECONOMY

Agricultural Products: beef cattle, catfish, chickens, corn, cotton, eggs, peaches, peanuts, pecans, soybeans, strawberries

Manufactured Products: chemicals, clothing, fertilizers, food products, paper products, steel, textiles, wood products

Natural Resources: coal, crushed stone, limestone, marble, natural gas, oil, oyster, shrimp

Business and Trade: finance, shipping, real estate, wholesale and retail trade

CALENDAR OF CELEBRATIONS

Eagle Awareness Weekends Throughout January, bird lovers gather at Lake Guntersville State Park to watch magnificent bald eagles soar overhead.

Mardi Gras Mobile is home to the nation's oldest Mardi Gras celebration. Each February the town cuts loose with two weeks' worth of parades and revelry.

Rattlesnake Rodeo The highlight of this March festival in Opp is the world's only rattlesnake race. You can also enjoy games, arts and crafts, and educational programs about rattlesnakes.

Battle of Selma Reenactment Each April, history buffs in Selma bring the Civil War's Battle of Selma to life.

Alabama Jubilee Hot Air Balloon Festival Colorful hot air balloons fill the sky during this May festival in Decatur.

Blessing of the Fleet Everyone in the fishing center of Bayou Le Batre comes out for this May event, which features a parade of boats, oyster-schucking and crab-picking contests, pet shows, and much seafood to eat. Seafood gumbo is especially popular.

Hank Williams Sr. Day Fans from across the nation flock to the tiny town of Georgiana each June to hear the songs of the country music legend at his boyhood home.

W. C. Handy Music Festival Each August, Florence celebrates the music of the Father of the Blues with a week filled with jazz, blues, and gospel concerts.

Cherokee Pow Wow and Green Corn Festival At this event honoring the

W. C. Handy Music Festival

region's Native Americans, you'll hear rhythmic music, watch vibrant dancing, and admire tepees and jewelry. The celebration takes place in Turkeytown in September.

Tennessee Valley Old-Time Fiddlers Convention Come to Athens in October for a weekend of toe-tapping music. In addition to fiddle contests, the convention also features harmonica, banjo, mandolin, and guitar competitions.

Gulf Shores National Shrimp Festival More than 200,000 people descend on Gulf Shores in October to walk the sandy beaches and eat their fill of seafood. They might also enjoy music, arts booths, and a sand sculpture contest.

National Peanut Festival George Washington Carver, the man who invented peanut butter, spoke at the first National Peanut Festival in 1938. Today, this November event in Dothan features peanut recipe contests, livestock shows, and lots of fun and games.

Christmas on the River Each December in Demopolis, a glowing parade of boats decorated with lights brightens the night as they travel down the Tombigbee River.

STATE STARS

Hank Aaron (1934–   ), a Mobile native, holds the Major League record for career home runs. He passed Babe Ruth's legendary record of 714 in 1974 and ended his career with 755. He is also the all-time Major League leader in runs batted in, extra base hits, and total bases. Aaron spent most of his career with the Braves, at first in Milwaukee and later in Atlanta. A quiet, consistent player, he led the league in home runs 4 times and hit at least 30 in a season 15 times. During his long career, he played in 24 all-star games. Aaron was elected to the National Baseball Hall of Fame in 1982.

Ralph Abernathy (1926–1990) was a Baptist minister and civil rights leader who was Martin Luther King Jr.'s closest associate in the 1950s and early 1960s. Together they led the Montgomery bus boycott and helped found a civil rights organization called the Southern Christian Leadership Conference (SCLC). Abernathy was president of the SCLC from 1968 until 1977. He was born in Linden.

Tallulah Bankhead (1903–1968), an actress born in Huntsville, was the daughter of William Bankhead, a Democratic politician who eventually became the Speaker of the U.S. House of Representatives. Bankhead left school at 15 and moved to New York, where she quickly established herself as a brilliant theater actress. The New York drama critics named her the year's best actress for *The Little Foxes* in 1939 and *The Skin of*

Tallulah Bankhead

Our Teeth in 1942. Although she never enjoyed the same success in movies, with her raspy voice and sophistication, she made her mark in films such as *Lifeboat*.

Hugo Black (1886–1971), a U.S. Supreme Court justice, was a native of Harlan. Black became a lawyer and was eventually elected to the U.S. Senate. In 1937, he was appointed to the Supreme Court, where he became known for his unwavering support of personal liberties such as freedom of speech.

Paul "Bear" Bryant (1913–1983) was the most successful college football coach in history. Bryant, who was born in Arkansas, attended the University of Alabama, where he later became an assistant coach. He coached at Maryland, Kentucky, and Texas A&M before settling in as head coach at Alabama from 1958 to 1982. Legendary for being strict and demanding, Bryant was also extremely successful. By the end of his career, he had racked up 323 victories, more than any other college coach.

Truman Capote (1924–1984) was an elegant, poetic writer famous for such novels as *Breakfast at Tiffany's*, about a lively New York playgirl. Many people think his greatest triumph was what he called his "nonfiction novel," *In Cold Blood*. It is a dark and disturbing account of a multiple murder in a small Kansas town. Capote, who was born in New Orleans, Louisiana, and spent his early years in Monroeville, Alabama, often delved into his southern background in his writing.

George Washington Carver (1864–1943) was a botanist who spent much of his career at Alabama's Tuskegee Institute. Carver, who was born in Missouri, became the director of the Department of Agricultural Research at Tuskegee Institute, a school for blacks in Tuskegee, Alabama, in 1896. Carver spent the rest of his life there doing agricultural research. He discovered hundreds of products that could be made from such local plants as sweet potatoes and peanuts, including peanut butter. He also developed a better type of cotton and ways to improve soil.

George Washington Carver

Nat King Cole (1919–1965) was a singer, beloved for his smooth, rich voice.

Cole was an outstanding jazz pianist of the 1940s. In 1944, his Nat King Cole Trio had its first big hit with "Straighten Up and Fly Right." Later hits included "Mona Lisa" and "Unforgettable." In the 1940s, Cole was the only African American with his own commercial network radio show, and in 1956 he became the second black to have his own national television program. He was born in Montgomery.

Nat King Cole

William Crawford Gorgas (1854–1920), a doctor born in Mobile, was a pioneer in the control of such deadly diseases as yellow fever, malaria, and bubonic plague. Gorgas joined the army and in 1898 was sent to Havana, Cuba, to try to control a yellow fever epidemic. He was not able to control the epidemic until it was understood that the disease was spread by mosquitoes. By eliminating places where mosquitoes could breed, Gorgas freed Havana from the disease. He later did the same thing in Panama, where disease was slowing the construction of the Panama Canal.

W. C. Handy (1873–1958) was a composer and trumpet player known as the Father of the Blues. Handy began his career as a performer and a teacher. By 1907, he had begun composing. While traveling through the Mississippi Delta, Handy heard the blues for the first time. He later wrote such classics as "Saint Louis Blues" and "Beale Street Blues," which brought the blues its first international recognition. Handy grew up in Florence.

W. C. Handy

Helen Keller (1880–1968) was an author and lecturer who lost both her sight and her hearing before age two. Eventually, her teacher, Anne Sullivan, found ways to teach her to communicate. Keller learned to read Braille, to write with a special typewriter, and to speak. After graduating from Radcliffe College in 1904, she became an advocate for the blind and people with other disabilities. The play *The Miracle Worker* is based on her life. Keller was born in Tuscumbia.

Martin Luther King Jr. (1929–1968) was the preeminent leader of the civil rights movement of the 1950s and 1960s, renowned for promoting nonviolent protest. King was born in Atlanta, Georgia, and became a Baptist minister. In 1954, he became a pastor at a church in Montgomery, Alabama, where he began his career as a civil rights leader. King's mesmerizing speaking, idealism, and dignity made him a national figure. In 1957, he helped found the Southern Christian Leadership Conference, a leading civil rights organization. He is perhaps best remembered for his "I have a dream" speech during the 1963 March on Washington. King, who won the 1964 Nobel Peace Prize, was assassinated in 1968.

Harper Lee (1926–) is a writer whose only novel, *To Kill a Mockingbird*, earned a Pulitzer Prize and was made into a successful movie. The book, which is set in a small Alabama town much like Lee's native Monroeville, concerns a lawyer who is defending a black man accused of a crime he didn't commit. The novel was acclaimed for dealing with ideas about prejudice and heroism while also providing an insightful look at southern culture.

Joe Louis (1914–1981), who was born in Lafayette, was the world heavyweight boxing champion from 1937 to 1949. In 1936, Louis, who was nicknamed the Brown Bomber, lost to German Max Schmeling. The Nazi regime in power in Germany at the time viewed Schmeling's victory as evidence of the superiority of whites. But when Louis beat Schmeling in a rematch in 1938, Americans celebrated, and Louis became an inspirational figure during World War II. During his career, Louis won 68 of his 71 bouts.

Joe Louis

Willie Mays (1931–   ), who was born in Westfield, is perhaps the greatest baseball player ever. Mays began his career with a bang, leading the New York Giants to the 1951 National League pennant, earning the Rookie of the Year Award, and winning legions of fans with his hustle and intelligence. Remarkably versatile, Mays was the first player to hit 300 home runs and steal 300 bases in his career. He ended his career with 660 home runs, the third-highest career total. An amazing center fielder, Mays was famous for his spectacular catches and exceptionally strong and accurate throws. In 1964, Mays became the first African-American captain of a Major League team. He was elected to the National Baseball Hall of Fame in 1979.

Alexander McGillivray (1759?–1793) was a Creek Indian leader whose father was Scottish and mother was Creek and French. Born near what is now Wetumpka, he spent his early childhood with the Creeks before being educated with whites in South Carolina. A skilled diplomat, McGillivray worked to unite the various Indian nations against white settlers, who were taking more and more of their land.

Jesse Owens (1913–1980), a legendary track and field star, set 11 world records during his career. In one incredible afternoon in 1935, he broke three world records and tied another. At the Olympics in Berlin, Germany, the following year, Owens won four gold medals—in the 100-meter dash, the 200-meter dash, the long jump, and the 400-meter relay—embarrassing the German leader Adolf Hitler, who believed that whites were superior to blacks. Owens was born in Oakville.

Jesse Owens

Satchel Paige (1906–1982) was one of the greatest pitchers in baseball history. When Paige began playing ball, African Americans were barred from the Major Leagues, so Paige spent most of his career in the Negro Leagues. Paige's power and consistency are legendary. It is said that in 1934, he won 104 out of 105 games. Paige didn't get the chance to play in the Major Leagues until 1948, when he was more than forty years old. That year he joined the Cleveland Indians, leading them to a World Series victory. Paige, who was elected to the National Baseball Hall of Fame in 1971, was born in Mobile.

Rosa Parks (1913–   ) was a civil rights activist who set off the Montgomery bus boycott in 1955, when she was arrested after refusing to give up her seat on a bus to a white passenger. As a result of Parks's case, the U.S. Supreme Court ruled segregation on public transportation unconstitutional. Parks was born in Tuskegee and attended Alabama State Teacher's College. She became active in the National Association for the Advancement of Colored People, a leading civil rights organization, and in 1943 became the secretary of the Montgomery branch. After the boycott, Parks stayed active in the civil rights movement.

Julia Tutwiler (1841–1916) was a social reformer who fought for girls' education and for prison reform. She helped establish girls' schools and convinced the University of Alabama to admit women. She also wrote the words to the Alabama state song. Tutwiler was born in Greene Springs.

Robert Van de Graaff (1901–1967) was a physicist who invented a particle accelerator that is used in nuclear physics. The Van de Graaff generator has also been used in medicine to treat cancer. Van de Graaff was born in Tuscaloosa and attended the University of Alabama.

George Wallace (1919–1998), a four-term Alabama governor, was born in Clio. During his first term as governor, Wallace became famous for his support of racial segregation. In 1963, he personally tried to block black students from entering the University of Alabama. Wallace ran for president as an independent in 1968 on a platform opposing desegregation and won in five states. In 1972, while again campaigning for president, he was shot and became paralyzed. In later years, Wallace changed his position on segregation.

Booker T. Washington (1856–1915) was the most prominent African American of the late 19th century. Washington had been born a slave in Virginia. After the Civil War, he attended the Hampton Institute in Virginia, where he later became a teacher. In 1881, he was hired to organize Tuskegee Institute, a vocational college for blacks in Alabama. At the school, Washington emphasized practical training that would land African Americans jobs. Washington promoted a conservative view about civil rights, arguing that blacks needed to improve themselves through economic self-reliance and job skills before they could be given equal rights. He remained president of Tuskegee until his death.

Dinah Washington (1924–1963), an exceptionally versatile jazz and blues singer, was born in Tuscaloosa. Washington could use her high, clear voice to express desperate sadness, rousing joy, and every emotion in between. She had her biggest hit in 1959 with "What a Difference a Day Makes."

Dinah Washington

Hank Williams (1923–1953) was one of the greatest and most influential country music singers ever, famous for such songs as "I'm So Lonesome I Could Cry" and "Your Cheatin' Heart." Williams was born in Mt. Olive. While still a teenager, he was already leading a popular band in Montgomery. In 1949, his first performance at the Grand Ole Opry went over so well that he sang six encores. With their direct lyrics expressing intense emotions, his songs dominated the country music charts for the next few years. But Williams led a troubled life, suffering from alcoholism and other problems. He died of a heart attack at age 29.

TOUR THE STATE

Birmingham Civil Rights Institute (Birmingham) The moving history of African Americans' struggle for equal rights is told at this museum using film, music, and storytelling.

Birmingham Civil Rights Institute

Alabama Sports Hall of Fame (Birmingham) This site is filled with memorabilia from the careers of Jesse Owens, Joe Louis, Hank Aaron, and many other Alabama sports greats.

Birmingham Zoo Look a Siberian tiger in the eye, watch golden spider monkeys cavort, and admire how elegantly huge polar bears glide through the water at one of the largest zoos in the Southeast.

Ave Maria Grotto (Cullman) This strange and fascinating site contains miniature replicas of 150 churches and shrines from throughout the world. A monk named Brother Joseph Zoettl built them over the course of 50 years using everything from semiprecious stones to soup cans.

Wheeler National Wildlife Refuge (Decatur) More than 300 bird species pass through this refuge at some point during the year. Telescopes have been set up so you can see the birds without frightening them away. The refuge also includes pleasant walking trails and picnic spots.

U.S. Space & Rocket Center (Huntsville) The world's largest space museum is also the most visited tourist site in Alabama. You can wander among rockets and other spacecraft, watch films taken by astronauts in space, and take a bus tour through NASA's Marshall Space Flight Center, where you might see mission control and space shuttle test sites.

Ivy Green (Tuscumbia) At the childhood home of Helen Keller, you'll hear the extraordinary story of how she learned to communicate despite being blind and deaf. You'll even see the pump where she learned her first word, *water.*

Alabama Music Hall of Fame and Museum (Sheffield) Exhibits, recordings, and memorabilia tell the story of great Alabama musicians, from Hank Williams to Nat King Cole.

W. C. Handy Home and Museum (Florence) Here you can see the log cabin where the Father of the Blues was born, along with handwritten music, photographs, and the piano on which he composed "St. Louis Blues."

Russell Cave National Monument (Bridgeport) Nine thousand years ago, ancestors of modern Native Americans lived in this cave in northeastern Alabama. Today, you can view the cave and some of the pottery, tools, and other artifacts that have been found there.

DeSoto State Park (Fort Payne) This park features a spectacular scenic drive, hiking trails, and the lovely 100-foot-tall DeSoto Falls.

Horton Mill Covered Bridge (Gadsden) This picturesque bridge is 70 feet above the Black Warrior River. No other covered bridge in the nation crosses as high above the water.

Gaineswood (Demopolis) One of the most beautiful mansions in the South, this house boasts a ballroom with gigantic columns and mirrored walls, glass domes in the ceiling, and its original furnishings.

Dexter Avenue King Memorial Baptist Church (Montgomery) Martin Luther King Jr. became a national figure while he was pastor at this church during the 1950s. A highlight of the church tour is a mural that depicts events in King's life and the civil rights movement.

First White House of the Confederacy (Montgomery) Jefferson Davis and his family lived in this house in the early days of the Confederacy, before the capital was moved to Richmond, Virginia. Today it houses items that once belonged to the Davis family and furnishings from that era.

Bellingrath Gardens and Home (Theodore) These gorgeous gardens include more than 250,000 azalea plants, as well as camellias, water lilies, dogwoods, and so many other flowering plants that there are always spectacular blooms, no matter what the season.

Gulf State Park (Gulf Shores) Miles of white sand beaches lure sunbathers, while the waters beckon swimmers, fishing enthusiasts, and surfers. The park also boasts freshwater lakes perfect for fishing and canoeing and trails through pine forests that appeal to hikers and bikers.

Fort Morgan (Gulf Shores) This star-shaped fort was built in the early 19th century and remained in use through World War II. Besides touring the fort, you can visit its museum, which is filled with military artifacts.

U.S.S. *Alabama* (Mobile) Exploring this World War II battleship will give you a feel for what life was like for its crew of 2,500.

FUN FACTS

Peanut butter was invented by George Washington Carver at Tuskegee Institute in Tuskegee, Alabama.

You might think the people of Enterprise in southeastern Alabama would hate the boll weevil after the insect destroyed two-thirds of the region's cotton crop in 1915. But instead they erected a monument to the boll weevil, because it forced them to grow other crops, including peanuts and corn, which brought the region greater prosperity.

In 1910, the world's first flying school was established in Montgomery by aviation pioneers Wilbur and Orville Wright.

Although today Mardi Gras is more associated with New Orleans, the first Mardi Gras celebration in North America began in Mobile in 1703.

FIND OUT MORE

You can find out a lot more about Alabama at your local library or on the Internet. Here are a few suggestions to get you started:

GENERAL STATE BOOKS

Davis, Lucile. *Alabama.* New York: Children's Press, 1999.

Fradin, Dennis Brindell. *Alabama.* New York: Children's Press, 1998.

SPECIAL-INTEREST BOOKS

Davidson, Margaret. *Helen Keller.* New York: Scholastic, 1997.

Lee, Harper. *To Kill a Mockingbird.* New York: Warner Books, 1960.

McKee, Jesse O. *The Choctaw.* New York: Chelsea House, 1989.

Parks, Rosa. *I Am Rosa Parks.* Illustrated by Wil Clay. New York: Dial Books, 1997.

Rennert, Richard. *Henry Aaron.* New York: Chelsea House, 1994.

Solomon, Jack, and Olivia Solomon. *Ghosts and Goosebumps: Ghost Stories, Tall Tales and Superstitions from Alabama.* Athens: University of Georgia Press, 1994.

Wills, Charles A. *A Historical Album of Alabama*. Brookfield, CT: Millbrook Press, 1995.

Yelverton, Mildred G. *They Also Served: 25 Remarkable Alabama Women*. Ampersand Publishing, 1993.

RECORDINGS

Handy, W. C. *W. C. Handy's Memphis Blues Band*. Memphis Archives.

Louvin Brothers. *Tragic Songs of Life*. Capitol.

Sun Ra. *Monorails and Satellites*. Evidence Music.

Williams, Hank. *The Original Singles Collection*. Mercury.

ONLINE RESOURCES

www.archives.state.al.us

This is the official online register of the state of Alabama. It includes basic historical information about the state, descriptions of government offices, and up-to-date lists of government officials, as well as many facts and statistics about the state.

www.newsdirectory.com/travel.al

This is a thorough and easy-to-use directory of information on cities, parks, historical landmarks, and other interesting sites in Alabama.

INDEX

Page numbers for charts, graphs, and illustrations are in boldface.